The
Effective
Invitation

The *Effective* Invitation

A Practical Guide for the Pastor

R. Alan Streett

kregel
PUBLICATIONS

Grand Rapids, MI 49501

The Effective Invitation by R. Alan Streett.

Copyright © 1984 by R. Alan Streett.

Published in 1995 by Kregel Resources, an imprint of
Kregel Publications, P. O. Box 2607, Grand Rapids, MI
49501. Kregel Resources provides timely and relevant resources for Christian life and service. Your comments and
suggestions are valued.

Cover Design: Alan G. Hartman

Library of Congress Cataloging-in-Publication Data
Streett, R. Alan (Richard Alan)
  The effective invitation / R. Alan Streett.
      p.   cm.
  Originally published: Old Tappan, N.J.: Fleming H.
Revell Co., c1984.
  Includes bibliographical references and index.
  1. Evangelistic invitations. I. Title.
BV3793.S678   1995   265'.9—dc20   95-11719
                                            CIP

ISBN 0-8254-3788-1 (paperback)

        3 4 5 6 7 printing / year 05 04 03 02 01

Printed in the United States of America

Dedicated to
"My three sons"
Aaron, Daniel, and Andrew

Who will one day grow up and read these pages. May
this book be a vehicle divinely used to lead
you into a lifetime of evangelism.

"Every believer should realize that no matter what
his employment is, it is only paying his expenses
to be an ambassador for the Lord Jesus Christ."
James A. Stewart

Acknowledgments

The Effective Invitation, although researched and written entirely by the author, was a collective effort on the part of many individuals. It is my express joy to acknowledge these dear saints of God.

Dorothy Drinkwater typed the complete manuscript and put it in a form acceptable for publication. Thanks, Dorothy!

A special "thank you" is also extended to Clarence Hottel and the members of the Baltimore Breakfast Group, who saturated me with prayer as I collected data, interviewed evangelists, and wrote the book. If *The Effective Invitation* is used by God to bring many into the kingdom, it will be the result of these fervent prayers.

Additionally, I wish to thank Sterling Huston and Elwyn Cutler, Billy Graham team members, for their parts in arranging my personal interview with Billy Graham; and to Dr. Graham, who consented to the meeting despite a demanding schedule.

I wish to especially thank and acknowledge my wife, Lynn, who continually encouraged me to press on until the research and writing of this book were finished. She was also responsible for proofreading the finished manuscript several times.

Finally, to the host of others—too numerous to mention—who answered evangelistic questionnaires, pointed me to obscure and ancient reference works, and who offered constructive criticism, thank you. I hope you feel a sense of accomplishment in seeing this book in print.

Contents

Motivational Theme • Call to Public Commitment
How You Can Deliver an Effective Invitation: Voice
Quality • Other Characteristics

Delayed-Response Invitation: The After Meeting
• Special Appointments • Signing of
Cards • Special Classes • Delayed Altar
Call • Dangers
Immediate-Response Invitation: The Altar
Call • Raising of Hands and Standing at the
Seat • Act of Public Confession • Progressive
Invitation • Baptism • The Private Deci-
sion • Dangers
Importance of Counseling: Ministry of Personal
Workers • The Inquiry Room

How Music Has Been Used to Win Souls
Functions of Music in Evangelistic Preaching

The Gospel Appeal to Children
How to Present the Message to Children:
Call to Repentance and Faith • Extending the
Invitation

Introduction

If you are a preacher, I guarantee and promise and avow that you will like *The Effective Invitation* immensely and profoundly.

Each one of us will find himself vitally interested in any subject dear to the heart. If a man is interested in money, he will find himself drawn to any discussion about how to accumulate wealth. If a man is interested in farming, he will unconsciously gravitate toward those who specialize in agriculture. It is so with medicine. It is so with law. It is so with merchandising. It is so with any interest in life. This generalization is particularly and especially true with regard to the calling of the ministry of Christ. The preacher cannot but find himself basically drawn to a study that concerns the proclamation of the gospel and the winning of the lost. That is why I so assuredly avow that any preacher, anywhere, will be blessed by the study of the public invitation presented in this book.

It is my own deep and everlasting persuasion that the preacher is not an ornament, nor is he an embellishment, nor is he a superfluous figure. The preacher is the man of God pointing the way to heaven. As such, the proclaimer of the gospel ought to preach for a verdict. Moses did. Isaiah did. Jesus did. Peter did. Paul did. Every great preacher of the everlasting hope in Christ has no less poured his life into that appeal that the lost be saved. For a man to preach just for the sake of preaching is a travesty on the truth of God. We ought to preach with a purpose and plead for a response.

It would be unthinkable that an insurance salesman would talk to a client and forget to ask him to sign on the dotted line. This observation is true in every area of life. The man in the store is to sell his wares to his customers. The real estate man is to present the property in such a way that the contract is accepted. When the lawyer stands before the jury, he is pleading for a verdict; the life of his client depends upon it. This is eminently and preeminently true of the preacher. He is pleading for a verdict that will change the destiny of his hearer from hell to heaven and his life from empty vanity to everlasting purpose and meaning.

We who are preachers have a heavenly assignment. We are to rescue the perishing. We are to win souls for the Savior. We are to present the gospel of Christ in such a way that men convicted by the Holy Spirit and drawn to the atoning grace of Christ are delivered from sin and presented one day faultless before the presence of God's glory. This is the meaning of the invitation, and this is the purpose of this splendid book by Dr. Streett. There is no preacher on the earth but will be blessed by these pages. With all my heart, I commend it to the emissary of God wherever he stands to proclaim the saving grace of our Lord.

W. A. Criswell
Pastor's Study
First Baptist Church
Dallas, Texas

Preaching must move the will if it is to change lives through the grace of God. For this reason, the final test of any sermon is what people do about it. The content of the message is prevented from degenerating into mere rationalism on the one hand, and mere emotionalism on the other hand, by the way it is linked with commitment.

Truth by its nature demands a verdict. Thus, insofar as God's Word comes through, response is expected. One cannot hear a clear presentation of Scripture and remain indifferent. If it is understood, then it must be obeyed. This is true of all preaching, but it is especially crucial when holding forth the good news of salvation.

The Cross does not permit the luxury of neutrality. There can be no compromise. Heaven and hell are in the balance. A sermon that does not convey this urgency lacks evangelistic relevance. Through the human instrumentality of the invitation the servant of the Word, in reliance upon the Holy Spirit, should do everything possible to move the hearer to take the right course of action.

Yet, strangely, at this point many able ministers feel awkward. Too often, I am afraid, nothing has been done to prepare them for this responsibility. Even in seminary homiletics classes the public invitation may be given only cursory attention, or passed over altogether. It is one of those sacred areas where not angels, but professors, fear to tread.

That is why this volume comes as a welcome resource. It addresses the need to call people publicly to Christ. The whole subject is put in biblical and historical perspective. Significantly, too, helpful counsel is offered as to how the invitation can be handled, describing the pros and cons of different approaches. Believing that one will find here a wealth of practical information and encouragement, I take pleasure in commending it to you.

Robert E. Coleman, Ph.D.
Director
School of World Mission and Evangelism
Trinity Evangelical Divinity School
Deerfield, Illinois

Preface

Every preacher and teacher of God's Word should plan opportunities to preach the gospel and extend an invitation for unbelievers to commit their lives publicly to Christ. Only as the man of God delivers the good news accompanied with an ultimatum, can he say with the Apostle Paul, "I am pure from the blood of all men" (Acts 20:26). "It must be remembered," writes Professor C. E. Autrey, "that if a pastor fails to invite his listeners to accept Christ, he is departing from the practice of the New Testament church."[1]

In a survey conducted by *Psychology Today*, more people said they wanted eternal life than anything else.[2] The evangelical pastor is in a unique position to show the unregenerated how this can be obtained and to provide them with an immediate opportunity to receive it.

The public invitation is an important tool which can aid in leading people to Christ at the end of a gospel sermon. The ability to use this tool effectively cannot be discovered at a conference on evangelism, by reading a book on soul winning or attending weekly classes on new evangelistic techniques. It can only be gained through experience. The man who regularly issues an invitation, sets aside the necessary time for preparation and depends on the Holy Spirit for help will be the man who becomes adept in calling sinners to Christ. The old adages, "Experience is the best teacher" and "Practice makes perfect," apply to this specific skill. Through trial and error, success and failure, the ability to give an effective invitation is attained.

Dr. G. Campbell Morgan once told how he challenged a group of fellow ministers to carry on the work of evangelism faithfully in their respective communities. Dr. Morgan's exhortation came at the conclusion of an areawide evangelistic campaign. He said:

> The last meeting I held was with the ministers, a conference in which they asked what they could do to take up and carry on the work. I suggested that on the next Sunday night every man, whether he had ever done so before or not, should preach to his own congregation with the distinctive and avowed purpose of persuading many of them whom he loved, but who as yet had not yielded to Christ, to yield to Him at once. To this they agreed, and on the next Sunday night every minister preached to his own people an evangelistic sermon, held an after-meeting, and through all the city men and women were saved. I believe that every minister who would prayerfully hold such a service in his own church, and among his own people, would have actual and definite results.[3]

Dr. Morgan's advice should be seriously considered. If every minister who reads this book would only step out in faith next Sunday and issue a public invitation of some kind, a great harvest of souls would be gathered for the Lord. If the practice were extended for successive weeks, a mighty revival could sweep the land!

The
Effective
Invitation

1

Tell Me, What Is the Gospel?

One of the common errors committed by evangelical pastors is the practice of preaching a message devoid of the gospel content and then inviting the listeners to receive Jesus Christ as Lord and Savior. Famed British theologian John R. W. Stott, former rector of All Souls Church in London, England, writes that "we must never issue an appeal without first making the proclamation."[1] The proclamation of which he speaks is the gospel. He notes:

> Evangelistic preaching has too often consisted of a prolonged appeal for decision when the congregation has been given no substance upon which the decision is to be made. But the gospel is not fundamentally an invitation to men to do anything. It is a clear declaration of what God has done in Christ on the cross for their salvation. The invitation cannot properly be given before the declaration has been made. Men must grasp the truth before they are asked to respond to it.[2]

Stott is saying that the gospel message about Christ and the gospel invitation to receive Christ as Lord and Savior are not to be equated. Proclamation and invitation are the two distinct components of every gospel presentation. Although related to each other in the evangelistic process, the preaching of the gospel must always precede the call for listeners to respond to its truth. The Scottish divine, James A. Stewart, similarly remarks, "There is a danger, in our earnestness to win souls for Christ, of our giving the invitation before proclaiming the message."[3]

What ingredients make up an effective gospel presentation? For the answer one needs to look no further than the New Testament record. This inspired source book contains several Greek words which reveal the nature and content of the first evangelistic sermons.

Two families of words are used coextensively with apostolic preaching. The first cluster deals with the theme of "proclamation." The second group is associated with the theme of "evangelism."

Words Dealing with Proclamation

Three key words in the New Testament deal with the topic of proclamation: *kērygma, kēryssō,* and *kēryx.* Each sheds a different light on the meaning of this important concept.

Preaching

Kērygma, found eight times in the Greek New Testament, is translated "preaching" each time in our English versions. In his classic *The Apostolic Preaching and Its Developments,* the Oxford scholar, C. H. Dodd, writes, "Preaching . . . is the public proclamation of Christianity to the *non*-Christian world."[4] Pointing to the Apostle Paul's declaration to the Corinthians that "it pleased God by the foolishness of preaching to save them that believe" (1 Corinthians 1:21), Dodd notes, "The word here translated 'preaching,' *kērygma,* signifies not the action of the preacher, but that which he preaches, his message."[5]

In other words, *kērygma* is the content of the proclamation.

Based on a thorough study of the word *kērygma* as it is used throughout the New Testament, Dodd came to two further conclusions. First, the *kērygma* is fixed. By the time of the Apostle Paul's missionary journeys, all apostolic preaching contained at least the following:[6]

1. The prophecies were fulfilled, and the New Age was inaugurated by the coming of Christ.
2. Christ was born of the seed of David.
3. He died for our sins according to the Scriptures, to deliver mankind out of the present evil age.
4. Christ was buried.
5. He rose on the third day according to the Scriptures.
6. Christ was exalted to the right hand of God, as Son of God and Lord of the quick and the dead.
7. He will come again as Judge and Savior of men.

The fixed *kērygma* was never preached in a vacuum, but was proclaimed by the apostolic believers to the world around them to the end that sinful men would repent and trust Christ as their Savior.

Second, Dodd concluded that there was a major distinction between preaching (*kērygma*) and teaching (*didachē*).[7] The latter he defined as ethical teaching, apologetics or exposition of theological doctrine. It was normally addressed to believers, while the preaching (*kērygma*) was directed to unbelievers. If Dodd's observations were correct, much of what is defined as preaching in twentieth-century pulpits is really teaching.

Several reputable scholars have challenged Dodd's second conclusion. Dr. Robert Mounce is one who points out that the terms *didachē* and *kērygma* are sometimes used interchangeably in the four Gospels.[8] He explains that "teaching is the expounding in detail of that which is proclaimed."[9]

Since the *kērygma* is a declaration of facts about the Person and work of Jesus Christ, it is informational. This means a certain amount of teaching is inherent in preaching. The great doctrines of justification and reconciliation, for example, cannot simply be proclaimed. They must also be explained and defined for the hearer's understanding. As Charles Spurgeon said:

> The gospel is a reasonable system, and it appeals to man's understanding; it is a matter of thought and consideration, and it appeals to the conscience and the reflective powers. Hence, if we do not teach men something, we may shout, "Believe! Believe! Believe!" but what are they to believe? Each exhortation requires a corresponding instruction or it will mean nothing.[10]

Proclaim

Kēryssō, used sixty-one times in the text of the Greek New Testament, is a verb which means "to proclaim" or "to preach." While *kērygma* signifies the *content* of a proclamation, *kēryssō* is the *act* of preaching or declaring that message to a group of people. Thayer expands upon this definition and says *kēryssō* means "to proclaim after the manner of a herald; always with the suggestion of formality, gravity, and an authority which must be listened to and obeyed."[11] He points out that in the Christian context it is "used of the public proclamation of the gospel and matters pertaining to it."[12] Alan Richardson likewise notes: "The fundamental idea . . . is the telling of news to people who had not heard it before—'evangelization.'"[13] C. H. Dodd observes: "The verb 'to preach' frequently has for its object 'the gospel.' . . . It would not be too much to say that whenever 'preaching' is spoken of, it always carries with it the implication of 'good tidings' proclaimed."[14] For Dodd, the act of preaching is evangelization. In fact, he suggests that sermons which lack evangelistic content are not entitled to be called "preaching" in the New Testament sense of the word.

Preacher

Kēryx, a noun rendered "preacher" in its three appearances in the English New Testament, is used twice by the Apostle Paul to describe himself (1 Timothy 2:7; 2 Timothy 1:11). This Greek word literally means "a herald, a person who makes a public announcement on another's behalf."[15] Writes Dodd, "A *kēryx* may be a town crier, an auctioneer, a herald, or anyone who lifts his voice, and claims public attention to some definite thing he has to announce."[16] G. Campbell Morgan emphasizes that the message being delivered is a proclamation from the king.[17] The connotation is that of an ambassador or personal representative who serves as the king's spokesman or mouthpiece. J. I. Packer enlarges upon the idea of ambassadorship:

He is the authorized representative of a sovereign. He speaks, not in his own name, but on behalf of the ruler whose deputy he is, and his whole duty and responsibility is to interpret that ruler's mind faithfully to those to whom he is sent. Paul used this figure twice, both times in connection with his evangelistic work.[18]

The Apostle Paul saw himself as Christ's personal representative. To the Corinthian church he wrote, "For Christ *sent me* . . . to preach the gospel" (1 Corinthians 1:17 italics added). From a prison cell in Rome he requested of the Ephesians prayer "that utterance may be given unto me, that I may open my mouth boldly, to make known . . . the gospel, for which I am an *ambassador* in bonds" (Ephesians 6:19,20 italics added). He used this same title in pleading with the Corinthians: "Now then we are *ambassadors* for Christ, as though God did beseech you by us ... be ye reconciled to God" (2 Corinthians 5:20 italics added). In each instance the office of the emissary was linked to the preaching of the gospel.

The preacher (*kēryx*) is an evangelist. He is a herald of the gospel. He is an ambassador. As Christ's representative he has divine authority and, therefore, has the right to be heard. He actually speaks forth the Word of God, not his own.

The origin and nature of the proclamation are such that "the herald does not just preach good news, whether men will hear or whether they will forbear. No. The proclamation issues in an appeal. The herald expects a response."[19] Of the apostles, Roy Fish observes: "The very nature of the message they preached compelled them to appeal for response."[20]

Words Dealing with Evangelism

Three key words in the New Testament deal with the topic of evangelism: *evangelion, evangelizō* and *evangelistēs.* Each sheds new light on the meaning of this important concept.

Gospel

The noun *evangelion,* translated "gospel" seventy-seven times in the English New Testament, simply means good news. In the context of the Christian faith it signifies "the glad tidings of salvation through Christ."[21] *Evangelion* is a synonym for *kērygma.* This is clearly seen in Romans 16:25, where the Apostle Paul equates the two terms: "Now to him that is of power to stablish you according to my gospel (*evangelion*), and the preaching (*kērygma*) of Jesus Christ ... which was kept secret since the world began." *Evangelion,* then, speaks of the content of the message proclaimed.

James A. Stewart has analyzed seven scriptural titles directly associated with *evangelion,* each of which illuminates the gospel message.

1. "The gospel of God" (Romans 1:1).
Stewart writes:

> This speaks of its ORIGIN. It is God's gospel. It was born in the heart and mind of the Father. As Paul told the Galatians, it is not a man-made message. It is good news from Heaven. The gospel in a nut-shell is "For God so loved the world, that He gave His only begotten Son, that whosoever believeth in Him should not perish, but have everlasting life."   (John 3:16)
> The gospel is that "God was in Christ, reconciling the world unto HIMSELF."   (2 Corinthians 5:19)[22]

David Watson agrees, "It is both his initiative and his revelation. Man, left to himself, could neither find God nor know the truth about God. But God has graciously revealed Himself. It is therefore essentially God's gospel, not man's."[23]

Not only does the gospel originate with God, it also tells us about God. It speaks of an infinite, personal, loving God who desires to be a Father to man, and who sends His Spirit into the human heart to cry, "Abba, Father." Packer adds that the gospel tells man who God is, what He is like, what His standards are and what He requires:

> It tells us that we owe our very existence to Him, that for good or ill we are always in His hands and under His eye, and that He made us to worship and serve Him, to show forth His praise and to live for His glory. These truths are the foundation of theistic religion, and until they are grasped, the rest of the gospel message will seem neither cogent nor relevant.
> The gospel starts by teaching us that we, as creatures, are absolutely dependent on God, and that He, as Creator, has the absolute claim on us. . . . We must know what it means to call God Creator before we can grasp what it means to speak of Him as Redeemer.[24]

2. "The gospel of Christ" (Romans 1:16), also called "the gospel of our Lord Jesus Christ" (2 Thessalonians 1:8) and "the gospel of his Son" (Romans 1:9).

> These titles speak of the THEME of the gospel, which is the Person and work of our glorious Kinsman-Redeemer. Paul, in his introductory remarks to his great Gospel treatise to the church at Rome says, "Paul, a servant of Jesus Christ, called an apostle, separated unto the gospel of God . . . concerning his Son Jesus Christ our Lord."
>
> (Romans 1:1,3)[25]

The gospel is about Jesus Christ. But what about Him? The Apostle Paul reminded his Corinthian readers that he preached, "Jesus Christ *and* Him crucified" (1 Corinthians 2:2 italics added). His message was twofold. First, he spoke about the *Person* of Jesus Christ, His historical reality as well as His present ministry in heaven. Second, Paul preached the crucifixion event (the work of Christ): His atoning death, His burial, and resurrection to bring about man's salvation.

Dr. Packer warns that "we must not present the Person of Christ apart from his saving work."[26] This is the common error committed by most liberal pastors and theologians. It is not enough to talk about Jesus the teacher, Jesus the prophet, Jesus the healer or even Jesus the martyr. Such a message is not "the gospel of Christ." When Paul claims he was sent to preach the gospel (1 Corinthians 1:17), he identifies that message as "the preaching of the cross" (verse 18). That meant the entire crucifixion event.

> Moreover, brethren, I declare unto you the *gospel* which I preached unto you . . . how that Christ died for our sins according to the scriptures; and that he was buried, and that he rose again the third day according to the scriptures.   (1 Corinthians 15:1,3,4)

Paul's definition of the gospel includes three essentials. First, "Christ died for our sins according to the Scriptures" (v. 3). His death was a fulfillment of the Old Testament prophecies. He was God's Lamb who was sacrificed as a sin offering for the world (John 1:29). Second, "he was buried" (v. 4). This is proof that Christ was indeed dead. He did not swoon into some co-matose state, suspended between life and death, but actually experienced death's reality (Philippians 2:8; Hebrews 2:9). Finally, He "rose again the third day according to the scriptures" (v. 4). The resurrection of Christ is proof that God accepts His death as the final and supreme sacrifice for sin. Romans 4:25 speaks of Jesus, "who was delivered for our offences and was raised again for our justification." Stewart says, "The death of Christ was the payment for our sins, while the resurrection was the receipt."[27] The crucifixion event is the basis upon which a holy God can declare the guilty sinner to be righteous.

A second danger to be avoided when preaching the gospel is to "present the saving work of Christ apart from His Person."[28] This is often the error of evangelical pastors and theologians. Packer comments:

> In their concern to focus on the atoning death of Christ, as the sole sufficient ground on which sinners may be accepted with God, they have expounded the summons to saving faith in these terms: "Believe that Christ died for your sins." The effect of this exposition is to represent the saving work of Christ in the past, dissociated from His Person in the present, as the whole object of our trust. But it is not biblical thus to isolate the work from the Worker. Nowhere in the New Testament is the call to believe expressed in such terms. What the New Testament calls for is faith in (*en*) or into (*eis*) or upon (*epi*) Christ Himself; the placing of our trust in the living Savior, who died for sins. The object of saving faith is thus not, strictly speaking, the atonement, but the Lord Jesus Christ, who made the atonement. We must not in presenting the Gospel isolate the cross and its benefits from the Christ whose cross it was. For the persons to whom the benefits of Christ's

death belong are just those who trust His Person, and believe, not upon His saving death simply, but upon Him, the living Savior. "Believe on the *Lord Jesus Christ,* and thou shalt be saved," said Paul. "Come unto *Me* . . . and I will give you rest," said our Lord.[29]

Packer's point is an important one. Christianity is a relationship with the living Lord of the universe. So often evangelical preachers exhort their listeners to embrace the doctrine of the atonement rather than the Christ who offered His life as an atonement. The One who died as Savior has risen, and is Lord. Thus we preach "the gospel of our *Lord* Jesus Christ." As Stewart explains:

> The official title of our Redeemer is now "The Lord Jesus Christ," because of His resurrection and ascension. It is interesting to note that our Savior is called by His earthly name, Jesus, 608 times *before* His ascension, and only 62 times *after* His ascension; that while He is never mentioned as "The Lord Jesus Christ" before His ascension, He is called "The Lord Jesus Christ" 81 times after His ascension. It is also striking to notice that as the apostles preached the Lordship of the Redeemer, their listeners were cut to the heart and bowed in surrender to Him.[30]

Peter's sermon on the day of Pentecost centered on the lordship of Christ. He proclaimed, "Therefore, let all the house of Israel know assuredly that God hath made this same Jesus, whom ye have crucified, both Lord and Christ. Now when they heard this, they were pricked in their hearts" (Acts 2:36,37).

Likewise, when the Apostle Paul preached at Corinth, he proclaimed Jesus as the exalted Lord: "For we preach not ourselves, but Christ Jesus the *Lord*" (2 Corinthians 4:5 italics added).

Our task as evangelists is to reproduce as faithfully as possible this New Testament emphasis. As James Denney points out:

> We do not think of separating [Christ's] work from Him who achieved it. The New Testament knows only a living Christ, and all apostolic preaching of the gospel holds up the living Christ to men. But the living Christ is Christ who died, and He is never preached apart from His death, and from its reconciling power. It is the living Christ, with the virtue of His reconciling death in Him, who is the burden of the apostolic message. . . . The task of the evangelist is to preach Christ . . . in His character as the Crucified.[31]

The job of the preacher is to point people to the crucified and risen Lord and call upon them to trust in Him.

3. "The glorious gospel of Christ" (2 Corinthians 4:3,4).

This title emphasizes the gospel's intrinsic worth and majesty. Stewart comments, "It is a glorious gospel because it is a gospel of the glory of the Redeemer."[32]

Scripture relates that the preexistent Son of God, who shared the glory of His Father (John 17:5), came to earth in the form of a man and veiled His glory behind human flesh (Philippians 2:6,7). Only once was His glory manifested, on the Mount of Transfiguration in front of the disciples Peter, James, and John (Matthew 17:2; John 1:14; 2 Peter 1:17,18). Paul reminds his friends at Philippi that "being found in fashion as a man, he humbled himself, and became obedient unto death, even the death of the cross" (Philippians 2:8). To the Corinthians, Paul writes, "But we speak the wisdom of God in a mystery . . . which none of the princes of this world knew: for had they known it, they would not have crucified the Lord of *glory*" (1 Corinthians 2:7,8 italics added). At His resurrection, Christ's inner glory broke through the veil of flesh and was manifested to the disciples (Luke 24:37; 1 Peter 1:11).

The gospel is also glorious because of the benefits the person who believes its message will receive. Not only does the believer become a recipient of eternal life (John 3:16); he also is given the glory of God in his heart (2 Corinthians 4:6). In His high priestly prayer, Jesus declared to His Father, "And the glory which thou gavest me I have given them" (John 17:22). The believer *in* Christ receives the glory *of* Christ.

At the rapture of the church, the believer's body which was purchased at Calvary (1 Corinthians 6:20) will be changed and likened to His glorious body (1 Corinthians 15:51–53; 1 John 3:3). Thus, the believer's salvation will be complete.

4. "The gospel of the grace of God" (Acts 20:24).

"This title describes . . . the CHARACTER of the Evangel," says Stewart.[33] The gospel is good news about God's grace. Such a message presupposes the bad news about man's sin. The depravity of the Adamic race makes the message of grace necessary. Human need is the background. Man is a sinner, and deserves eternal punishment in hell. On the basis of Christ's atoning death, and according to God's grace, the Father offered man forgiveness of sins. General William Booth, founder of the Salvation Army, once described great preaching as "preaching damnation with a cross at the center of it."[34] This is the gospel of grace.

No one can work for or earn his salvation. It is a free, unmerited gift, issuing forth from the heart of God (Ephesians 2:8,9). Paul stresses that all believers are "justified freely by his *grace* through the redemption that is in Christ Jesus" (Romans 3:24 italics added).

5. "The gospel of peace" (Ephesians 6:15).

Peace is the FRUIT of the gospel. The Scripture declares, "Therefore being justified by faith, we have *peace* with God through our Lord Jesus Christ" (Romans 5:1 italics added). This peace was established through the death and resurrection of the Son of God (Romans 4:24,25). Paul observes that we have "peace through the blood of his cross" (Colossians 1:20). To the Ephesians he writes, "Ye who sometimes were afar off are made nigh by the blood of Christ. For he is our peace" (Ephesians 2:13,14). The prophet Isaiah foresaw the price of this peace: "But he was wounded for our transgressions, he was bruised for our iniquities. The chastisement of our peace was upon him; and with his stripes we are healed" (Isaiah 53:5). The Cross of Calvary produces peace for the believer. The message, therefore, is a gospel of peace.

6. "The gospel of your salvation" (Ephesians 1:13).

This title speaks of the individual APPROPRIATION that must be made. Until the hearer believes the facts of the gospel and receives Jesus Christ as his own personal Lord and Savior, the gospel message offers no hope for salvation.

The death of Christ does not automatically bring about a universal salvation; rather, it establishes the basis upon which God can show mercy to all who believe. "For he hath made him to be sin for us, who knew no sin; that we *might* be made the righteousness of God in him" (2 Corinthians 5:21 italics added), says Paul. The Apostle Peter agrees: "For Christ also hath once suffered for sins, the just for the unjust, that he *might* bring us to God, being put to death in the flesh, but quickened by the Spirit" (1 Peter 3:18 italics added). The gospel message must be personally embraced. As the title suggests, it should be "the gospel of *your* salvation."

7. "My gospel" (Romans 2:16).

It is not until "God's gospel" (the first title examined) becomes "my gospel" that the enterprise of evangelizing a lost and dying world can be accomplished. Each believer is commissioned to be a bearer of the good news. He becomes a fellow worker with God in fulfilling the Great Commission (Matthew 28:18–20; 2 Corinthians 6:1). The Apostle Paul speaks of the "glorious gospel of . . . God, which was committed to *my* trust" (1 Timothy 1:11 italics added). To possess the gospel brings with it a divine obligation to proclaim it. Hence, the great apostle cries, "Necessity is laid upon me; yea, woe is unto me, if I preach not the gospel" (1 Corinthians 9:16).

When "God's gospel" becomes "my gospel," a spiritual revolution occurs!

Evangelize

The Greek verb *evangelizō* is used fifty-five times in the New Testament. It means "to bring good news" or "to announce glad tidings." In the Septuagint translation of the Old Testament, it is used to describe "a runner coming with the news of victory; in the Psalms it occurs twice in the sense of proclaiming God's faithfulness and salvation."[35] It signifies the act of preaching the good news that the battle for men's souls has been won by Christ at Mount Calvary (John 12:31–33; Colossians 2:13–15; Hebrews 2:14,15; 1 John 3:8).

The verbs *evangelizō* and *kēryssō* are similar in meaning, the only difference being the direction of action. *Kēryssō* speaks of being sent by the king with a message. *Evangelizō* places the emphasis on the act of bringing to others the message.

Evangelist

The Greek noun *evangelistēs,* used three times in the Greek New Testament, appears in most English translations as "evangelist." The word means "a bringer of good tidings," and has basically the same meaning as *kēryx.*

The evangelist is a specially gifted person given to the church by the ascended Lord for the purpose of numerically building the church and training others for a similar ministry (Ephesians 4:8–12). Morgan defines the evangelist's special calling:

> A man who receives the gift of the evangelist is one to whom there is given a clear understanding of the evangel, a great passion in his heart results from the clear vision, a great optimism fills his soul, born of the confidence in the

power of Christ to save every man; and growing out of that passion and confidence a great constraint seizes him to tell somebody, to tell everybody the glad news of salvation by Jesus Christ. Those peculiar qualities are not found in all men called to the ministry. . . . But where this is the all consuming fire, there you have an evangelist.[36]

Two persons are specifically assigned the title "evangelist" in the New Testament. The first is Philip (Acts 21:8), a deacon in the church at Jerusalem (Acts 6:5), who had an itinerant ministry throughout the regions of Samaria and Caesarea (Acts 8:5–40).

The title is also extended to Timothy, the overseer of the church at Ephesus, whom the Apostle Paul told to "do the work of an evangelist" (2 Timothy 4:5). From these references it is possible to conclude that the gift of the evangelist can operate within or beyond the local assembly of believers. The evangelist Philip was sent out from the church at Jerusalem to minister in other cities and provinces. Timothy, on the other hand, did his evangelizing mostly within the local church setting.

While most pastors agree on the necessity of evangelizing the lost world, many are hesitant to perform a ministry of evangelism in their own congregations. Paul urged Timothy to "do the work of an evangelist," and thus "make full proof of thy ministry" (2 Timothy 4:5). "The clear implication of this passage," says Lewis A. Drummond, "is that a pastor cannot fulfill his ministry unless he fulfills his role as evangelist."[37] Kenneth S. Wuest believes that the local pastor, like Timothy, "should be evangelistic in his message and methods. He must ever be reaching out for the lost both in his teaching, preaching and personal contacts."[38] The reason is obvious. Every local assembly has worshipers who are lost (1 Corinthians 14:23). The organized church is a great mission field. That is why Professor Smeaton of Edinburgh told his theology students, "Gentlemen, reckon your ministry a failure unless souls are won to Christ."[39] John Wesley exhorted his circuit-riding preachers, "You have only one business, and that is the salvation of souls."[40] Morgan remarks:

> No church ought to be allowed to exist that has not added to its membership by confession of faith. If a church is existing only by letters of transfer, it is time the doors were closed, and "Ichabod, the glory of the Lord has departed" was inscribed across them.[41]

Every local church needs to utilize the ministry of a God-called, God-equipped evangelist. In addition, the pastor must do the *work* of an evangelist, and thus fulfill his ministry. Every pulpiteer should heed the admonition of G. Campbell Morgan:

> Therefore I submit that the minister of Jesus Christ ought occasionally to hold meetings where he urges immediate decisions, and gives the opportunity for the same. We must not be led astray from the essential work of the Christian ministry by imagining we have some gift that does not include within it something of the evangelistic necessity, or urging the claim of Christ upon individuals. I hold no regular ministry is complete in which there is never an opportunity for immediate decision on the part of those who are brought into contact with the fact of the lordship of Christ, and who hear the evangel of salvation.[42]

2
The Theological Content of the Invitation

Just as some evangelical preachers give an invitation without first proclaiming the gospel, so others preach the gospel without issuing an appeal for the hearers to act upon the message. All evangelistic sermons recorded in the Book of Acts include both proclamation and invitation. The purpose of the *kērygma* was to show sinful men their need of forgiveness and salvation through Jesus Christ. Conversion of the lost was the objective of first-century preaching. The gospel was never declared "as a matter of mere academic interest," notes James H. Jauncey. "Clearly, the hearer was being challenged by it to believe and commit his life to Christ in faith."[1] The message always had a personal application to the listener.

The invitation is that act by which the preacher of the gospel exhorts his hearers and instructs them how to appropriate the content of the *kērygma* in their individual lives. Any sermon that does not include an invitation as well as a proclamation is not New Testament-style preaching. Every sermon should aim to stir the human will. Truth is something that must be obeyed. It is the gospel invitation that presses home the claims of Christ and calls for an immediate response.

John R. W. Stott's exhortation to the twentieth-century church is an important one:

> We must never make the proclamation without then issuing an appeal. . . . We are to find room for both proclamation and appeal in our preaching if we would be true heralds of the King. . . . It is not enough to teach the gospel; we must urge men to embrace it.[2]

"When the nature of the gospel is examined," notes Fish, "it is obvious that it represents an offer. God makes man a concrete offer of forgiveness of sin on the basis of the saving acts of his Son. Such an offer demands a decision."[3]

James A. Stewart similarly remarks:

> The sinner is required to hearken and respond to the message or perish. Imbedded in the word "evangelism" is the thought of the messenger waiting to know what answer to take back to Him by whom he was sent. The gospel cannot be ignored. The true evangelist must demand an answer. He cries out like Moses, "I call heaven and earth to record this day against you, that I have set before you life and death, blessing and cursing; therefore choose life!" (Deuteronomy 30:19). The messenger of God must not be content merely to preach a delightful sermon. He must breathlessly await the answer to God's ultimatum.[4]

"Though preaching is done primarily in the indicative mood, that is, stating the facts about Jesus, the imperative mood calling for a response is also there,"[5] writes Fish.

In his "Yale Lectures on Preaching" in 1911, John Henry Jowett concluded, "In all our preaching we must preach for verdicts. We must present our case, we must seek a verdict, and we must ask for immediate execution of the verdict."[6]

Three times the New Testament records the heart-cry,

"What must we do?" following a proclamation (Luke 3:10; Acts 2:37, 16:30). Every gospel message should raise this same question in the hearts and minds of its hearers, and every effective invitation should answer this inquiry of the hungry soul (Luke 3:11; Acts 2:38, 16:31). Simply instructing people to "come forward and receive Christ" does not adequately answer the query. Similar admonitions such as "raise your hand" or "stand at your seat" also fall far short of the New Testament invitational pattern. While these requests may have a place in an invitation, they should not constitute its main thrust. Apostolic invitations consisted mostly of instructions filled with theological content. The New Testament herald explained to his listeners what God expected of them in light of the message preached. He then urged them to heed God's command and be saved.

To discover what theological ingredients the invitation should contain, one has only to read Mark's account of Jesus' first public sermon: "Jesus came into Galilee, preaching the gospel of the kingdom of God, and saying, The time is fulfilled, and the kingdom of God is at hand: *repent* ye, and *believe* the gospel" (Mark 1:14,15 italics added).

Jesus' first discourse began with the *proclamation*, "The time is fulfilled, and the kingdom of God is at hand." Next came the *appeal:* "Repent ye, and believe the gospel." Repentance and faith were the two demands Jesus placed upon His hearers. Every listener was called upon to respond in this twofold manner.

Evangelistic sermons recorded in the Book of Acts exhibit a consistently similar pattern. In Acts 3:12–26, for example, Peter addresses a gathering of Jews near Solomon's Porch. After delivering the gospel (*kērygma*) "Ye men of Israel . . . ye delivered up [Jesus], and denied him in the presence of Pilate . . . ye denied the Holy One . . . and killed the prince of life, whom God hath raised from the dead" (v. 12–15), he then issues an appeal for his listeners to act upon the message: "Repent ye therefore, and be converted, that your sins may be blotted out" (v. 19).

In both Jesus' and Peter's sermons, repentance was the primary call for action, followed by an appeal to believe in the gospel. The preaching of the Apostle Paul manifested the same progression. When describing his evangelistic activity among the Ephesians, Paul stated that his sermons included both proclamation and invitation:

> I kept back nothing that was profitable unto you, but have showed you and have taught you publicly, and from house to house [proclamation], testifying both to the Jews, and also to the Greeks, repentance toward God and faith toward our Lord Jesus Christ [invitation]. (Acts 20:20,21)

Notice, Paul's invitation called upon people to repent and believe. Repentance he described as being "toward God." Since man's sin is basically an act of rebellion against the divine Sovereign of the universe (Psalms 51:4; Luke 15:18), he is called upon to show repentance toward Him. Faith, on the other hand, is specifically directed toward God's only begotten Son. It is on the basis of Christ's death and resurrection that God is able to extend mercy and forgiveness to sinful man. Only when the sinner recognizes this and trusts Christ alone to save him, can he be reconciled to his heavenly Father.

Repentance toward God and faith in the Lord Jesus Christ are the two steps every person must take to be saved. For this reason, every invitation should call upon hearers to take these required steps.

Repentance

The English verb "to repent" comes from the Greek word *metanoeō*, found thirty-four times in the New Testament, and means "to have a change of mind toward someone or something."[7] The primary connotation of repentance in the New Testament is not emotional, but rational. This immediately dispels two false notions that people may have about the nature of repentance, the first being that it is related to human sorrow, remorse, or tears. It is quite possible for an individual to exhibit these emotional qualities without ever coming to a state of repentance. This does not mean a person who repents cannot be sorrowful over his sins (2 Corinthians 7:10). It simply suggests that the two actions are not synonymous, nor necessarily related.

A correct understanding of repentance dispels a second error—that of confusing penance with repentance. Penance refers to religious ritual or duty that one must perform before he can receive forgiveness of sins. Repentance, on the other hand, signifies the willful inward change of mind, not an initial outward action. The sinner must be transformed inside-out, not vice versa.

In the Old Testament, the concept of repentance (Heb. *shub*) has to do with "turning back" or making an "about face" (1 Kings 8:47; Ezekiel 14:6, 18:30), whereas the New Testament word *metanoeō* emphasizes an inward decision or change of mind. When these two concepts are combined, a complete picture of biblical repentance emerges. An excellent example of repentance is found in Matthew 21:28,29: "A certain man had two sons; and he came to the first, and said, Son, go work today in my vineyard. He answered and said, I will not: but afterward he repented, and went." The son's change of mind led to a change of action.

The parable of the prodigal son (Luke 15:11–32) provides another clear example of biblical repentance. In this passage Jesus tells of a young man who requested of his father his portion of the family inheritance. Money in hand, the lad journeyed to a far country where he wasted his life and substance on the pleasures of sin. This lasted for a short season. When a great famine hit the land, the bankrupt youth was forced to find employment feeding a herd of swine. He not only fed them; he lived among them. The Lord then says, "He came to himself" (v. 17). He began to see things in a clearer light. He changed his mind about his father, his home, himself, his companions, and most of all his condition. He realized that his father's hired servants lived in luxury compared to his dismal life-style. He said, "I will arise and go to my father" (v. 18). This change of attitude led to a change of action. Jesus relates that the young man carried out his decision: "And he arose, and came to his father" (v. 20).

This case history pictures true repentance. First came the inward change of mind. This resulted in action—the turning back to father and home. Had the young man remained in the far country, his repentance would have been spurious.

Roland Q. Leavell defines repentance as a "reversal of one's thinking which will result in an alteration of one's way of living."[8] The inward change of mind precedes the outward change of direction.

The prophet Isaiah describes lost humanity as wandering sheep, "gone astray . . . everyone [turned] to his own way" (Isaiah 53:6). The only remedy for this dilemma is repentance. The prophet commands:

> Let the wicked forsake his way, and the unrighteous man his thoughts: and let him return unto the Lord [repentance], and He will have mercy upon him; and to our God, for he will abundantly pardon. For my thoughts are not your thoughts, neither are your ways my ways, saith the Lord.   (Isaiah 55:7,8)

Dwight L. Moody used to say, "Man is born with his back toward God. When he truly repents, he turns around and faces God."[9] As King David reminisced, "I thought on my ways, and turned my feet unto thy testimonies" (Psalms 119:59).

Derek Prince, Greek scholar and former professor of philosophy at Cambridge University, draws a word picture of sinful man's journey away from God and his subsequent volitional return:

> In his own natural, unregenerate, sinful condition, every man that was ever born has turned his back on God, his Father, and on heaven, his home. In this condition, each step that he takes is a step away from God and from heaven. As he walks this way, the light is behind him and the shadows are before him. The further he goes, the longer and darker the shadows become. Each step that he takes is one step nearer the end—one step nearer the grave, nearer hell, nearer the endless darkness of a lost eternity. For every man that takes this course, there is one thing that he must do first, one essential act that he must make. He must stop, he must change his mind, change his direction, turn back, turn around, face the opposite way, turn his back to the shadows and face toward the light. This first, essential act is called in the scripture "repentance." It is the first move that any sinner must make who desires to be reconciled with God.[10]

The first call the gospel preacher must give in his invitation is that of repentance.

The Call to Repentance in the New Testament

Matthew records, "In those days came John the Baptist, preaching in the wilderness of Judea, and saying, Repent ye: for the kingdom of heaven is at hand" (Matthew 3:1,2). Notice the progression: first, John preached; then he exhorted, "Repent ye." The call to repentance followed the proclamation. Jesus' first preaching mission (in Matthew 4:17, parallel passage to Mark 1:15) followed the identical sequence: "From that time Jesus began to preach, and to say, Repent: for the kingdom of heaven is at hand." First, He preached (*kēryssō*). Second, He issued an appeal to repent.

Repentance was not the message of the gospel, but the initial response God expected from the hearers of the gospel. In one of His dialogues with the Pharisees, Jesus replied, "For I am not come *to call* the righteous, but sinners to repentance" (Matthew 9:13 italics added). The verb "to call" is *kaleō* and is directly linked to the act of inviting. *Kaleō* is the word used to describe the actions of the king's servants who were sent "to bid" guests to the wedding feast (Matthew 22:3,4).

The apostles also called upon their hearers to repent. As Peter finished proclaiming the gospel on the day of Pentecost, the multitudes cried out, "What must we do?" (Acts 2:37). Peter responded, "Repent!" (Acts 2:38). A call to repentance concludes Paul's famous sermon on Mars Hill: "God . . . now commandeth all men everywhere to repent" (Acts 17:30). When the preacher extends the invitation, it is God who is actually issuing the call for men to repent. The call is, in reality, a command; it is in the imperative mood. All apostolic sermons contained an appeal for repentance (*see* Acts 3:19, 20:21, 26:20).

The appeal to repent was made by preachers *before* Pentecost, *at* Pentecost, and *after* Pentecost. It is an indispensable element of every gospel invitation.

The Origin of Repentance

Repentance originates with God. "The goodness of God," writes Paul, "leadeth thee to repentance" (Romans 2:4). The psalmist spoke of God's role in repentance when he said, "Turn us again, O Lord . . . and we shall be saved" (Psalms 80:19).

Repentance is a gift from God. Speaking before the Sanhedrin, Peter testified: "The God of our fathers raised up Jesus, whom ye slew and hanged on a tree. Him hath God exalted with his right hand to be a Prince and a Savior, for *to give re-pentance* to Israel, and forgiveness of sins" (Acts 5:30,31 italics added).

Repentance is a gift for all peoples, for all times. Peter shared with his fellow apostles how God worked in the hearts of Cornelius's household: "When they heard these things, they held their peace, and glorified God, saying, Then hath God also to the Gentiles granted repentance unto life" (Acts 11:18). The Apostle Paul pointed out to young Timothy the source of repentance:

> And the servant of the Lord must not strive; but be gen-tle unto all men, apt to teach, patient, in meekness in-structing those that oppose themselves; if God peradventure will give them repentance to the acknowl-edging of the truth.   (2 Timothy 2:24,25)

Unregenerate man, apart from God's grace, cannot of his own volition repent of sin and turn to Christ in faith. Jesus said, "No man can come unto me, except the Father which hath sent me draw him" (John 6:44). When the preacher of the gospel calls for men to repent, he calls for them to do the hu-manly impossible. But he extends the invitation anyway, knowing that it has been preceded by the preaching of the *kērygma,* which is the power of God to save (1 Corinthians 1:18). As Packer says, "God works by His Spirit through His Word in the hearts of sinful men to bring them to repentance and faith."[11] Jesus reminded His audience that "the men of Nineveh . . . repented at the preaching of Jonah" (Luke 11:32). When the man of God has been faithful to preach the pure gospel, he can extend the invitation for sinners to repent, with the assurance that the Holy Spirit will work in the listeners' hearts (John 16:8). Prince remarks:

> For this reason, the supreme crisis of every human life comes at the moment of the Spirit's drawing to repen-

tance. Accepted, this drawing leads us to saving faith and eternal life; rejected, it leaves the sinner to continue on his way to the grave and the unending darkness of an eternity apart from God.[12]

The Relationship between Repentance and Faith

The question might rightfully be asked, "If repentance is so important, why do so many passages dealing with salvation omit it?" For example, the Gospel of John was written for the express purpose that men "might have life through his name" (John 20:31); yet the word "repentance" is not found once in the text. (The key word in John's Gospel is *believe.*) Often the Apostle Paul mentions only "faith" or "belief" as the criterion for salvation (*see* Acts 16:31; Ephesians 2:8,9).

Does this mean that it is not necessary to repent in order to be saved?

On the contrary. There can be no true faith that does not first involve a change of mind about sin, self, God, and Jesus Christ. Repentance is always a necessary ingredient of saving faith. True faith includes repentance.

That the terms repentance and faith are used interchangeably at times can be clearly seen by comparing John 3:16 with 2 Peter 3:9. John indicates that "whosoever believeth in him should not perish." Peter, on the other hand, makes repentance the requirement for not perishing: "The Lord is not . . . willing that any should perish, but that all should come to repentance." Therefore, to believe in Christ carries with it the idea of repentance, and the call to repent implies a turning in faith to Christ.

Repentance and faith are two sides of the same coin. This reciprocal relationship is seen in 1 Thessalonians 1:9 where Paul reminds his readers, "Ye turned to God from idols." Before one can turn *to God* (faith), he must first turn *from idols* (repentance). Repentance and faith are two aspects of the same action. Together they form the process known as conversion.

There is a danger, however, in inviting men simply to believe or to repent without properly defining the terms. So many people profess a faith in Jesus Christ that was not initiated by repentance. This results in a false faith or an easy-believism that does not save. On the other hand, some have an emotional experience falsely interpreted to be repentance that does not culminate in faith. Like Judas who "repented himself" (Matthew 27:3), these individuals are lost. Prince warns, "True repentance must always precede true faith. Without such repentance, faith alone must always be a mere empty profession."[13] As Morgan admonishes:

> We have been preaching "Believe," and we have not sufficiently said "Repent, repent, repent," and we still have to preach this truth. . . . There is no question of precedence. The quality of faith must be that of repentance, and the dynamic of repentance must be that of faith.[14]

Whenever these two terms are mentioned together, and not used as synonyms, repentance is always listed *first*. Jesus called upon His listeners to "repent and believe" (Mark 1:15). Paul spoke of "repentance toward God, and faith toward our Lord Jesus Christ" (Acts 20:21). The writer of Hebrews, in his list of foundational truths, first mentions "repentance from dead works," followed by "faith toward God" (Hebrews 6:1).

When issuing a gospel invitation, the preacher has two options. First, he may wish to call upon his listeners simply to "believe on the Lord Jesus Christ." In utilizing this method, it is essential that he clearly explain the full nature of saving faith. Or second, he may decide to call his listeners to conversion by outlining the two steps of repentance and faith individually, defining each more narrowly. In either situation, sinners must be made aware that God calls them to turn from their old ways and turn to His way, Jesus Christ.

Faith

The second response God expects from the sinner who hears the gospel is "faith" or "belief." Just as He commands men to repent (Acts 17:30), He also calls them to believe on the Son of God: "This is his commandment, that we should believe on the name of his Son Jesus Christ" (1 John 3:23).

The verb *pisteuō* is translated "believe," "commit," and "trust" 242 times in the English New Testament, and means "to rely on a person or thing."[15] Other shades of meaning include to have complete confidence in, to be fully persuaded, to be totally convinced, to cast oneself upon, to rest upon, and to wholly trust and commit. Richardson says, "To believe is to hold on to something firmly, with conviction and confidence."[16]

The noun form, *pistis*, is translated "faith" in all its New Testament usages. In relation to salvation, faith has for its object, the Person and work of Jesus Christ (John 6:29, 14:1; Acts 16:31; Romans 3:24,25). Wuest defines saving faith as "a definite taking of one's self out of one's own keeping and entrusting one's self into the keeping of the Lord Jesus Christ."[17] Packer's definition is similar: "to trust wholly in Christ and the power of His redeeming blood to give ... acceptance with God."[18]

Francis Schaeffer tells the following story which illustrates the biblical meaning of faith.

> A missionary when seeking a native word for faith could not find it. Finally, he sat in a chair and raised his feet from the ground, putting his full weight on the chair and bearing none of the weight himself. He then asked what word described his act, and used that word for faith. This is an accurate picture.
>
> Faith in Christ is resting totally on Him and His finished work.[19]

The Origin of Faith

Like its counterpart, repentance, faith is a gift from God. Man cannot of his own initiative produce faith. He can only receive it. This truth is evident from Paul's statement to the Philippians: "For unto you it is given in the behalf of Christ . . . to believe on Him" (Philippians 1:29). Peter opens his second epistle with these words: "Simon Peter, a servant and an apostle of Jesus Christ, to them that have obtained like precious faith with us through the righteousness of God and our Savior Jesus Christ" (2 Peter 1:1). The writer of Hebrews describes Jesus as "the author and the finisher of our faith" (Hebrews 12:2).

Faith is produced in the hearts of those who listen receptively to the gospel: "Faith cometh by hearing, and hearing by the word of God" (Romans 10:17). A. T. Robertson translates the last portion of the verse, "the word about Christ."[20] As the righteousness of Christ is offered to sinners through the Word, the Spirit of God produces faith in their hearts to respond positively.

As an ambassador of Christ, the preacher of the gospel concludes his message by inviting his hearers to be reconciled to God (2 Corinthians 5:20). At this junction the hearer must make a choice. Will he receive the offer of salvation by placing his faith in Jesus Christ, or will he spurn it? While the promise of eternal life is revealed through the proclamation, it can only be received through faith.

> He that believeth on him is not condemned: but he that believeth not is condemned already, *because he hath not believed* in the name of the only begotten Son of God.
>
> He that believeth on the Son hath everlasting life: and he that *believeth not* the Son shall not see life; but the wrath of God abideth on him (John 3:18, 36 italics added).

Like the prodigal son, the sinner may say, "I will arise and go to my father, and will say unto him, Father, I have sinned against heaven, and before thee" (Luke 15:18). Faith is a personal response of the heart. It is a volitional act. No one can exercise it on behalf of another. Each person must make the decision for himself. As one commentator says:

> Many are lost at this point, wishing to be saved and wanting to be saved. But wishing and wanting cannot save anybody. There must be a response, a choice, a decision. No one will be saved apart from a responsible, personal decision.[21]

An Examination of Hebrews 11:1

The eleventh chapter of Hebrews, known as the faith chapter in the New Testament, begins with a declaration about the nature of faith: "Now faith is the substance of things hoped for, the evidence of things not seen" (Hebrews 11:1). From this single verse several observations can be drawn. First, faith differs from hope. Hope is primarily related to the future, while faith is related to the present. "Faith *is.*" "He that believeth on me," said Jesus, "hath everlasting life" (John 6:47).

Second, faith is described as "substance" and "evidence." The late Donald Grey Barnhouse, one of this century's foremost Bible teachers, explained:

> When God tells us that faith is the substance of things hoped for He is conveying the title deed to us. And just here there is a wonderful lesson that can be brought out of the original language. When the New Testament was written, the Greek language of that day was being widely used down in Egypt. A few years ago a great many documents were discovered there in Egypt that were written in the very same dialect in which the New Testament was written, and in these papers the word that is translated substance is used repeatedly for title deed. There can be no doubt but that this is in keeping with God's definition of faith. Use that phrase. See how vivid it becomes. Now

faith is the title deed of things hoped for, the proof of things not seen. We believe God and He guarantees to translate our hopes into reality and to let us grip the invisible.[22]

Saving faith is substance because it has the Word of God for its foundation.

During the invitation, the preacher of the gospel calls upon his listeners to believe the testimony of God's Word. Those who respond positively are saved; those who do not remain lost. The reason man is lost is because he "hath made [God] a liar; because he believeth not *the record* that God gave of His Son" (1 John 5:10 italics added). Faith is taking God at His Word: "And this is *the record,* that God hath given to us eternal life, and this life is in his Son. He that hath the Son hath life; and he that hath not the Son of God hath not life" (1 John 5:11,12 italics added). Prince remarks:

> Scriptural faith does not consist in believing anything that we ourselves may wish or please or fancy. Scriptural faith may be defined as believing that God means what He has said in His Word—or again, as believing that God will do what He has promised in His Word to do.[23]

King David exercised faith when he said to the Lord, "Therefore now, Lord, let the thing that thou hast spoken concerning thy servant and concerning his house be established for ever, and do as thou hast said" (1 Chronicles 17:23). Rahab the harlot displayed faith when she responded to the spies' promise of delivering her family by saying, "According unto your words, so be it" (Joshua 2:21). The virgin Mary gave a similar response of faith when learning she was to give birth to the promised Messiah. She said, "Be it unto me according to thy word" (Luke 1:38).

> That is the secret of scriptural faith—"according to thy word." Scriptural faith is produced within the soul by the

hearing of God's Word, and then is expressed by the active response of claiming the fulfillment of that which God has said.[24]

Faith is more than mental assent (James 2:14). It comes to birth in a surrendered heart. It changes "can be saved" to "will be saved."

A final observation is that faith deals with "things not seen." Faith does not focus on the visible world. Rather, it is placed in God who is unseen, and in the crucifixion and resurrection of Jesus Christ that have taken place in history—all outside of man's present experience. Paul reminded his friends at Corinth, "For we walk by faith, not by sight" (2 Corinthians 5:7). To Thomas, the lone apostolic doubter of the resurrection, Jesus said, "Blessed are they that have not seen, and yet have believed" (John 20:29). Barnhouse comments:

> The world has a motto which says, seeing is believing. This comes from our dealings with men. . . . Men do not always make their promises good. The race has learned that it is necessary to proceed slowly and not trust men beyond a certain point. A man's reputation may be good, but his banker will most probably demand a good collateral before a loan is made. The performance has not always followed the promise, so the world says, seeing is believing.
>
> God tells us that when we deal with Him, believing is seeing. In the Gospel of John, the Lord Jesus Christ spoke to Martha at the graveside of her brother, Lazarus, and the Lord Jesus proclaimed the eternal principle of the working of faith. "Said I not unto thee . . . that if thou wouldest believe, thou shouldest see the glory of God?" In spiritual matters the believing must always precede the seeing. Now this is logical because we are dealing with God. He has never made a promise that has not been fulfilled.[25]

Abraham is the best example of saving faith in "things not seen." God promised to make Abraham the father of many nations (Genesis 12:3). Although both Abraham and his wife were well past ninety years of age, and childless, the Scripture says, "He believed in the Lord; and he counted it to him for righteousness" (Genesis 15:6). Despite the testimony of his senses, Abraham stood on the Word of God. The Apostle Paul, commenting on this event, writes:

> And being not weak in faith, he considered not his own body now dead, when he was about a hundred years old, neither yet the deadness of Sarah's womb: He staggered not at the promise of God through unbelief; but was strong in faith, giving glory to God; And being fully persuaded that, what he had promised, he was able also to perform. (Romans 4:19–21)

Abraham believed without seeing. He displayed true faith. From the moment he received God's promise, he believed it would come to pass. Abraham's faith resulted in salvation (Romans 4:22). Paul uses the truth of Abraham's encounter with God as a pattern of faith to be followed by all:

> Now it was not for his sake alone, that it was imputed to him; But for us also, to whom it shall be imputed, if we believe on him that raised up Jesus our Lord from the dead; who was delivered for our offences, and was raised again for our justification. (Romans 4:23–25)

A faith which is exercised on the basis of the promises of God alone, apart from feeling or seeing, is biblical faith. It results in imputed righteousness and justification for the believer.

3

The Public Invitation—Is It Biblical?

The first-century gospel preacher always concluded his evangelistic sermon with an appeal for the unconverted present to repent of their sins and place their faith in the crucified and resurrected Lord of glory. Often these appeals called upon the individuals additionally to demonstrate their sincerity by taking a public stand for Christ before friends, relatives, neighbors, and even enemies. This call for the sinner or new convert to make an initial public profession of faith is the basis for the modern-day practice of extending a public invitation.

Two types of public invitation were used in New Testament times. The first called for sinners to demonstrate publicly their desire to repent and believe, and was used as a means of bringing them to a state of conversion. The second called upon new converts, who had been supernaturally transformed by the message, openly to witness to their new-found faith.

The Call to Sinners

After Adam committed the first sin in the Garden of Eden, he tried to hide from God (Genesis 3:8). He did not succeed. God searched him out and called to him, "Adam . . . where art thou?" (Genesis 3:9). Only as Adam responded to that call and stepped out into the open could God clothe him with the righteousness provided through the blood sacrifice of an animal (Genesis 3:21). To remain hidden would have meant to remain unforgiven. Obedience to the invitation issued by God was essential if salvation was to be granted.

From the beginning of human history to the present, God has continued to extend an invitation to the lost to respond openly to His offer of forgiveness. The pages of both the Old and New Testaments are replete with examples of God, through His chosen servants, calling men to make a public commitment of faith.

Moses' descent from Mount Sinai was one such dramatic occasion. The children of Israel, impatient for their leader to return from his mountain-top visit with God, built an idol of gold (Exodus 32:1) to which they bowed down and paid homage (Exodus 32:4–6):

> And it came to pass, as soon as he came nigh unto the camp, that he saw the calf, and the dancing: and Moses' anger waxed hot, and he cast the tables out of his hands, and brake them beneath the mount. And he took the calf which they had made, and burnt it in the fire, and ground it to powder, and strawed it upon the water, and made the children of Israel drink of it. . . . Then Moses stood in the gate of the camp, and said, Who is on the Lord's side? Let him come unto me. And all the sons of Levi gathered themselves together unto him.   (Exodus 32:19,20,26)

Only those who obeyed the command of Moses and publicly stepped forward received an atonement for their sins (Exodus 32:30).

Joshua, Moses' successor, issued a similar public appeal when he said, "Choose ye this day whom ye will serve; . . . but as for me and my house, we will serve the Lord" (Joshua 24:15). This clear-cut invitation was made during a mass gathering of the nation (Joshua 24:1), and resulted in a united response:

> And the people answered and said, God forbid that we should forsake the Lord, to serve other gods. . . . The Lord our God will we serve, and his voice will we obey. So Joshua made a covenant with the people that day . . . and wrote these words in the book of the law of God, and took a great stone, and set it up there under an oak, that was by the sanctuary of the Lord. And Joshua said unto all the people, Behold, this stone shall be a witness unto us.
>
> (Joshua 24:16,24–27)

The Book of First Kings records another classic example of a public invitation. Here the prophet Elijah confronts the rebellious children of Israel who had forsaken God to worship Baal: "And Elijah came unto all the people, and said, How long halt ye between two opinions? If the Lord be God, follow Him, but if Baal, then follow him. And the people answered him not a word" (1 Kings 18:21).

Elijah called for the people to make a public response, but they gave none. Yet the invitation still stood. Like an urgent call which cannot go unanswered, it surfaced again in Elijah's intercessory prayer, God's lightning response, and the people's belated reaction:

> Hear me, O Lord, hear me, that this people may know that thou art the Lord God, and that thou hast turned their heart back again. Then the fire of the Lord fell, and consumed the burnt sacrifice. . . . And when all the people saw it, they fell on their faces: and they said, The Lord, he is the God; the Lord, he is the God. (1 Kings 18:37–39)

Only when the obstinate people saw a sign from heaven did they publicly respond to Elijah's original invitation to choose between God and Baal.

God constantly had to call the nation of Israel back to Himself, speaking through prophets and sometimes through kings, who issued a public decree for the people to repent and openly acknowledge allegiance to the Creator. One ruler He used for this purpose was King Josiah. Although Josiah's reign as king was an admirable one, he and his people fell into idolatry through ignorance of God's Word.

During the eighteenth year of Josiah's reign, the high priest of the temple discovered a hidden scroll containing the laws of God. After reading it, Josiah realized the great sin he and his people had committed in the sight of the one true God: "And it came to pass, when the king had heard the words of the book of the Law, that he rent his clothes" (2 Kings 22:11). After repenting of his own sin, he called a nationwide assembly to address his people:

> And the king sent, and they gathered unto him all the elders of Judah and of Jerusalem. And the king went up into the house of the Lord, and all the men of Judah and all the inhabitants of Jerusalem with him, and the priests, and the prophets, and all the people, both small and great: and he read in their ears all the words of the book of the covenant which was found in the house of the Lord. And the king stood by a pillar, and made a covenant before the Lord, to walk after the Lord, and to keep his commandments and his testimonies . . . with all their heart and all their soul, to perform the words of this covenant that were written in this book. And all the people *stood* to the covenant.   (2 Kings 23:1–3 italics added)

Josiah's call and the nation's public response brought revival to Judah. All the idols were destroyed, the false prophets and priests executed and the worship of God restored (2 Kings 23:4–24). Scripture records God's opinion of His servant Josiah: "And like unto him was there no king before him, that turned to the Lord with all his heart, and with all his soul, and with all his might, according to all the Law of Moses; neither after him arose there any like him" (2 Kings 23:25).

Others who called upon Israel to repent publicly and turn to God included Ezra (Ezra 10:1–5, 7–12), Nehemiah (Nehemiah 9:1–5,38) and Joel (Joel 2:1–17). None had greater success than Jonah, at whose preaching all the heathen people of Nineveh—from the greatest to the least—sat in sackcloth, fasted, and cried to God in repentance (Jonah 3:5–10).

Instances abound in the New Testament of people who felt the need to take public action in their quest for salvation.

Jesus publicly called to Himself the disciples of John the Baptist immediately after John's proclamation that Jesus was the Lamb of God (John 1:36). To two of the disciples—one of them Andrew—He said, "Come and see" (John 1:39). They did and were convinced by their visit that Jesus was the promised Messiah (John 1:41). The next day, He issued a similar appeal to Philip by saying, "Follow me" (John 1:43). While not specifically recorded, it is safe to assume that a similar public invitation was made to all His followers.

During His last visit to Jericho, Jesus met Zaccheus, who was perched in a tree trying to get a glimpse of the Savior:

> And when Jesus came to the place, he looked up, and saw him, and said unto him, Zaccheus, make haste, and come down, for today I must abide at thy house. And he made haste, and came down, and received him joyfully. And when they saw it, they all murmured, saying, That he was gone to be guest with a man that is a sinner.
>
> (Luke 19:5–7)

Three important facts are contained in this passage. First, Zaccheus was a sinner. Second, Jesus publicly issued an invitation for him to come down from the tree. Finally, Zaccheus responded in full view of a large crowd who knew him. It is obvious that Zaccheus considered the invitation a call to a changed life:

> And Zaccheus stood, and said unto the Lord; Behold, Lord, the half of my goods I give to the poor; and if I have taken anything from any man by false accusation, I restore him fourfold. And Jesus said unto him, This day is salvation come to this house.   (Luke 19:8,9)

The call for Zaccheus to make a public move toward the Savior and his obedience to that call are directly linked to his salvation: "And he made haste, and came down and *received* him joyfully." John 1:12 says, "But as many as *received* him, to them gave he power to become the sons of God, even to them that believe on his name." Zaccheus' coming down (public response) expressed his willingness to receive Christ (salvation).

Consider also the woman who had an issue of blood. She was healed of her disease the instant she touched the hem of Jesus' garment (Luke 8:44). But her salvation was not effected until after she publicly acknowledged her need and openly identified herself:

> And Jesus, immediately knowing in himself that virtue had gone out of him, turned him about in the press, and said, Who touched my clothes? And his disciples said unto him, Thou seest the multitude thronging thee, and sayest thou, Who touched me? And he looked round about to see her that had done this thing. But the woman fearing and trembling . . . came and fell down before him, and told him all the truth. And he said unto her, Daughter, thy faith hath *made thee whole;* go in peace.   (Mark 5:30–34)

"Made thee whole," the key phrase, is translated from the Greek word *sōzō* which is usually rendered "saved" throughout the New Testament. Thayer notes *sōzō* has the positive biblical meaning: "To make one a partaker of the salvation by Christ."[1] While the woman's healing was received in secret, her salvation was given after she openly responded to the Savior's inquiry. Her courage to step forward and confess her need was labeled by Jesus as "faith" and resulted in her reconciliation with God.

The thankful leper experienced a similar salvation. He and nine other lepers were completely healed physically (Luke 17:11–15), but only he returned to Jesus to express gratitude:

> And [he] fell down on his face at his feet, giving him thanks: and he was a Samaritan. And Jesus answering said, Were there not ten cleansed? But where are the nine? There are not found that returned to give glory to God, save this stranger. And he said unto him, Arise, go thy way: thy faith hath made thee whole. (Luke 17:16–19)

Again, an outward action—in this instance, falling at the feet of Jesus—is tied to saving faith.

Another example of a public confession related to faith and salvation is the case of the publican: "And the publican, standing afar off, would not lift up so much as his eyes unto heaven, but smote upon his breast, saying, God be merciful to me a sinner. I tell you, this man went down to his house justified" (Luke 18:13,14). The publican's acknowledgment of his dire spiritual condition took place in the temple, a public facility, in clear sight of onlookers. Jesus linked the man's actions and heartfelt cry to his salvation.

The conversion of the Philippian jailer also illustrates the need to demonstrate a public response to the gospel. Following an earthquake which he feared had set all his prisoners free, the jailer decided to kill himself (Acts 16:25–27). He stayed his hand, however, when he heard a familiar voice ring out in the darkness:

> But Paul cried with a loud voice, saying, Do thyself no harm: for we are all here. Then he called for a light, and sprang in, and came trembling, and fell down before Paul and Silas, and brought them out, and said, Sirs, what must I do to be saved? And they said, Believe on the Lord Jesus Christ, and thou shalt be saved, and thy house.
> (Acts 16:28–31)

The jailer sought salvation actively by going for help to those he knew to be men of God. Paul and Silas were then able to share the gospel with him and his family, and the whole household was saved (Acts 16:32–34). Similar scenes are reenacted daily as searching souls walk down church aisles or gather in front of an evangelist's platform to find eternal life. As counselors share God's Word with the inquirers, faith is born in the human heart.

Not every move toward Christ, of course, eventuates in salvation. Scripture relates the story of a rich young ruler who "came . . . running, and kneeled to him, and asked him, Good Master, what shall I do that I may inherit eternal life?" (Mark 10:17). Jesus immediately counseled the young man who, however, refused to act upon His advice "and went away grieved" (Mark 10:22).

Each of these case studies lends biblical support to the modern-day concept of the public invitation. Seekers responding to God's call should be dealt with, when possible, on an individual basis and have explained to them the full implications of what it means to repent and trust Christ alone for salvation.

The Gift of Exhortation

An examination of the gift of exhortation (Romans 12:8) furnishes convincing scriptural support for the practice of giving a public invitation. The word "exhort" comes from the Greek word *parakaleō*, used 108 times in the New Testament and variously rendered "beseech," "besought," "exhort," "entreat," and "called." *Parakaleō* (a combination of *para*, "to the side," and *kaleō*, "to call") is used in both classical Greek writings and the New Testament to mean, "to call to one's side, call for, summon." Corresponding with this writer, Dr. Paige Patterson, president of the Criswell Center for Biblical Studies, remarked on *parakaleō*:

I have frequently translated it as "give an invitation." Any time you come across the word "exhortation" on the pages of the New Testament, you have, in effect, an appeal made for people to come and stand with the speaker in whatever it is that he is doing. This of course could take many patterns, all the way from a silent acquiescence of the heart where one is standing or sitting, to the waving of a hand, or the actual presentation of the person before the congregation. In any case, it is an invitation to decide.[2]

Seen in this light, *parakaleō* would signify the call for people to come forward and stand by the preacher as an indication of their desire to repent of sin and believe on Jesus Christ.

Five times *parakaleō* is used in the New Testament in relation to evangelistic preaching. At the conclusion of his soul-winning sermon on Pentecost, Peter exercised the gift of exhortation to invite his listeners to respond publicly to the gospel:

> Then Peter said unto them, Repent, and be baptized every one of you in the name of Jesus. . . . For the promise is unto you, and to your children, and to all that are afar off, even as many as the Lord our God shall call. And many other words did he testify and *exhort* [*parakaleō*], saying, Save yourselves from this untoward generation. Then they that gladly received his word were baptized: and the same day there were added unto them about three thousand souls. (Acts 2:38–41)

If Dr. Patterson's definition of *parakaleō* is correct, Peter actually called for his listeners to respond publicly to his message by presenting themselves to him. The record makes it clear that Peter's invitation elicited an overt response, for approximately three thousand people openly indicated their desire to repent and submit themselves for baptism (v. 41).

Parakaleō occurs also in the ministry of Barnabas. In the face of persecution, many believers in Jerusalem were forced to scatter. As a result, the Word of God spread widely and multitudes came into a saving relationship with Christ (Acts 11:19–21). When news of the spiritual harvest filtered back, Barnabas was commissioned to go to Antioch and investigate (Acts 11:22): "Who, when he came, and had seen the grace of God, was glad, and *exhorted* [*parakaleō*] them all, that with purpose of heart they would cleave unto the Lord" (Acts 11:23). Barnabas, whose name means "exhorter," called the people to his side to the end that they would cleave to Christ.

A third occurrence of *parakaleō* is connected with the Apostle Paul's missionary activities among the people of Corinth. In inviting the Corinthians to be reconciled to God, Paul used the gift of exhortation: "Now then we are ambassadors for Christ, as though God did *beseech* [*parakaleō*] you by us: we pray you in Christ's stead, be ye reconciled to God" (2 Corinthians 5:20). Although Paul did the calling, it was as if God Himself gave the invitation. God and Paul worked together:

> We then, as workers together with him, *beseech* [*parakaleō*] you also that ye receive not the grace of God in vain. (For he saith, I have heard thee in a time accepted, and in the day of salvation have I succored thee: behold, now is the accepted time; behold, now is the day of salvation.)   (2 Corinthians 6:1,2)

Paul's invitation was given with urgency. He called on the people to respond immediately. Every evangelistic invitation, whatever the circumstances may be in which it is issued, should be characterized by a call for the hearer to take immediate action.

Parakaleō is also used by Paul in his charge to Timothy: "Preach the word [*kēryssō*]; be instant in season, out of season; reprove, rebuke, *exhort* [*parakaleō*] with all longsuffering and doctrine. . . . do the work of an evangelist, make full proof of thy ministry" (2 Timothy 4:2,5). The gift of exhortation is an invaluable asset to the gospel preacher. Kenneth O. Peterman writes that this gift includes "the ability to influence and to persuade others."[3] In sixty-one of its 108 appearances, *parakaleō* means "to beg or to plead" or "to express an urgent request." The evangelist or pastor possessing this gift is supernaturally endowed with an ability to persuade his listeners to respond publicly to the gospel message.

Paul counsels Timothy that his exhortations must be accompanied by longsuffering, or patience (2 Timothy 4:2). The term "longsuffering" is used by the Apostle Peter in relation to salvation: "The Lord . . . is longsuffering to us-ward, not willing that any should perish, but that all should come to repentance" (2 Peter 3:9). Exhortation is thus linked to repentance by longsuffering. As God waits patiently for sinners to repent, so must the pastor-evangelist persevere in extending the invitation. He must never give up.

Finally, the Apostle Paul includes the ability to exhort among the qualities to be desired in an elder: "For a bishop must be blameless . . . a lover of hospitality . . . holding fast the faithful Word as he hath been taught, that he may be able by sound doctrine both to *exhort* [*parakaleō*] and to convince the gainsayers" (Titus 1:7–9). Gainsayers were infiltrators of the church who claimed to be saved, but were actually reprobate (Titus 1:16). They were lost church members. They needed to be converted. The proclamation of the Word plus exhortation (invitation) would convince such unbelievers of their lost condition and lead them to repentance and faith. Invitations should be the rule of the day whenever the gospel is shared or preached.

The Use of the Word "Come"

Jesus often used the word "come" to call people to Himself. It was a form of exhortation. Those who publicly responded showed their desire for repentance and faith. In fact, the act was essential for salvation. Those who did not respond continued to walk in darkness. With the prideful Pharisees Jesus remonstrated, "Ye *will not come to me,* that ye might have life" (John 5:40).

The word "come" was first used as an invitation by God to bid Noah and his family enter the ark and escape divine judgment (Genesis 7:1). The ark was a type or picture of Christ, the ark of safety for the sin-weary soul. The invitation, "Come!", is extended to all who want to escape the wrath of God. It was in the context of future judgment that Jesus issued His great invitation: *"Come* unto me, all ye that labor and are heavy laden, and I will give you rest" (Matthew 11:28).

"Come" is last used as an invitation in Revelation 22:17: "And the Spirit and the bride say, Come. And let him that heareth say, Come. And let him that is athirst come. And whosoever will, let him take the water of life freely." In God's final invitation to lost humanity, a twofold appeal is given. First, the ascended Lord is invited to come and catch away the church. Second is the call for sinners, in the meantime, to come to Christ and receive life.

The invitation is issued by both the Spirit and the bride. The Spirit, of course, is God; the bride, the church. Here is a picture of God and man working together to bring the lost into the kingdom. As the evangelist or pastor extends the invitation for sinners to come to Christ, the Holy Spirit is also invisibly drawing them to the Savior.

Those invited are the thirsty. Jesus had made an identical offer in His discourse at the Feast of Tabernacles:

> In the last day, that great day of the feast, Jesus stood and cried, saying, If any man *thirst,* let him *come unto me,* and drink. He that believeth on me, as the scripture hath said, out of his belly shall flow rivers of living water. (But this spake he of the Spirit, which they that believe on him should receive. . . .) (John 7:37–39)

Jesus here equates the act of coming to Him with drinking, and drinking with believing. He alludes to the prophet Isaiah who previously had issued a similar appeal on God's behalf:

> Ho, every one that *thirsteth, come* ye to the waters, and he that hath no money; *come* ye, buy and eat; yea, *come.* . . . Incline your ear, and *come* unto me: hear, and your soul shall live; and I will make an everlasting covenant with you . . . Seek ye the Lord while he may be found, call ye upon him while he is near. Let the wicked forsake his way, and the unrighteous man his thoughts: and let him return unto the Lord, and he will have mercy upon him; and to our God, for he will abundantly pardon.
> (Isaiah 55:1,3,6,7)

The thirsty are invited to come to the Lord, a response equated with repenting and turning to God for mercy and pardon. John calls the thirsty, the "whosoever will" (Revelation 22:17).

Everyone who comes receives eternal life through Jesus Christ. They drink of "the water of life freely." This same promise was given the Samaritan woman at Jacob's well: "Whosoever drinketh of the water that I give him shall never thirst; but the water that I shall give him shall be in him a well of water springing up into everlasting life" (John 4:14).

Numerous times Jesus called people to come to Him. His general call was, "*Come,* take up the cross, and follow me" (Mark 10:21). To enter the kingdom required child-like faith: "Suffer little children, and forbid them not, to *come unto me:* for of such is the kingdom of heaven" (Matthew 19:14). Those who responded to His call were assured of a welcome: "All that the Father giveth me shall *come* to me; and him that *cometh* to me I will in no wise cast out" (John 6:37).

Entrance into the kingdom is similar to accepting a wedding invitation, as Jesus implied in His parable of the marriage dinner:

> The kingdom of heaven is like unto a certain king, which made a marriage for his son, and sent forth his servants *to call them* that were bidden to the wedding: and they would not come. Again, he sent forth other servants, saying, Tell them which are bidden, Behold, I have prepared my dinner: my oxen and my fatlings are killed, and all things are ready: come unto the marriage. But they made light of it, and went their ways.
>
> (Matthew 22:2–5)

Only those who respond positively to God's invitation can enter into the festivities. It is not enough to inwardly say, "I plan to attend" and then remain at home. Outward actions must match one's inward decision.

The "comes" of the New Testament were calls for young and old to make a physical and visible commitment to the Lord Jesus. As Christ called people to Himself then, so the gospel preacher today calls for people to take a public stand for Christ as an indication of their desire to receive Him as Lord and Savior. The public response is an exercise of the human will showing that the invitation to the marriage feast of the King's Son has been accepted.

Counting Converts

Further evidence that apostolic preachers called for public decisions for Christ was their ability to number their converts. The number of souls won to Christ on the day of Pentecost was calculated to be "about three thousand" (Acts 2:41). Soon after, another five thousand disciples were added to the ranks (Acts 4:4). As the gospel spread, the body of Christ grew: "And the Word of God increased; and the number of the disciples multiplied in Jerusalem greatly" (Acts 6:7). Many more were saved as "the hand of the Lord was with" the believers "and a great number believed, and turned to the Lord" (Acts 11:21). Samuel Fisk points out:

In all these instances the word used for "number" in the original is ARITHMOS, which can readily be recognized as a mathematical term. There seem to have been definite calculations of those who came to the truth, and these must have been based upon some outward, visible manifestation of their decisions.[4]

For converts to be countable, they had to be identifiable. There had to be some means of distinguishing the saved from the lost. Many references mention the quantity of converts, often using the word "multitudes" to describe the public response to the gospel (Acts 5:14; 6:1,7; 8:6,12; 10:44,48; 11:21, 24; 12:24).

Fishing for Souls

When Jesus said to His disciples, "Follow me, and I will make you fishers of men" (Matthew 4:19), He was drawing a word picture of soul winning. No knowledgeable fisherman simply throws in his line or net; he also must pull it in to make a catch. The act of pulling the fish out of the water and drawing it to the fisherman is a picture of the invitation. "Some will use only the rod and reel of personal evangelism," says L. R. Scarborough; "others must throw out and haul in the gospel net in public evangelism." He continues:

> The term "drawing the net" is applied to the preacher's invitation, at the close of his sermon, to the unchurched, the indifferent, and the unsaved to make a public response to the claims of Christ. It has reference to the destiny-determining action to be taken by those "fishing for men."[5]

As a fish must be removed from its natural environment, so the sinner drawn by the Spirit of God must be separated from his old, unbelieving way of life. Taking a public stand for Christ helps effect this transition.

Sowing and Reaping

Jesus likened lost mankind to a vast harvest field ready to be gathered by the hand of the reaper:

> Lift up your eyes, and look on the fields; for they are white already to harvest. And he that reapeth receiveth wages, and gathereth fruit unto life eternal: that both he that soweth and he that reapeth may rejoice together. And herein is that saying true, One soweth, and another reapeth. I sent you to reap that whereupon ye bestowed no labor: other men labored, and ye are entered into their labors.   (John 4:35–38)

On another occasion, Jesus challenged His disciples, "The harvest truly is plenteous, but the laborers are few; pray ye therefore the Lord of the harvest, that he will send forth laborers into his harvest" (Matthew 9:37,38).

Seed has been sown, obviously, in these fields. In order to have a harvest, there must first be a time of planting; in His parable of the soils, Jesus identifies the seed as the word of God—(Mark 4:14). As a result, a harvest has been produced. It is ready for the reaper. Jesus likens the harvest to a mass of conversion-ready souls waiting to be plucked for the Master. This is the job of the evangelist. No crop—not even the ripest vine-ready produce—can harvest itself. Laborers must be sent in to apply the sickle to the vines (Mark 4:29). Dr. J. Wilbur Chapman, who trained Billy Sunday to do the work of an evangelist, has observed:

> If a farmer were to occupy all his time in sowing the seed and make no provision for the gathering of a harvest which he would have a right to expect, we should think him bereft of all reason. There are certain laws governing the sowing of seed, the watching for growth and development and reaping of the harvest. It is likewise true that

> there are certain well-defined laws concerning the use of
> God's Word in teaching and preaching. . . . The responsi-
> bility for failure cannot be with the Lord of the harvest,
> but must be with those who are supposed to be the la-
> borers in His field. I can find no reason in God's Word
> why there should not be a constant ingathering . . . why
> there may not be frequent harvest seasons and oft-
> repeated decision days.[6]

The essential duty of the evangelistic preacher is to gather in
souls for Christ. As the seed (God's Word) is sown publicly, so
is the harvest to be reaped publicly. To sow only is to stop short
of the divine task and to leave the job undone. A public invitation is an integral part of the evangelistic process.

Finally, as the harvest is reaped fruit is gathered "unto life
eternal" (John 4:36). The promise is given that "in due season
we shall reap, if we faint not" (Galatians 6:9). A crop is
guaranteed. The psalmist put it this way: "They that sow in
tears *shall reap* in joy. He that goeth forth and weepeth, bearing precious seed, *shall doubtless* come again with rejoicing,
bringing his sheaves with him" (Psalms 126:5,6). Those who
have been faithful to the evangelistic task of calling conversion-ready souls (those "white to harvest") to a public commitment, have discovered the promise to be true. Much fruit has
been gathered "unto life eternal." Dr. Lee Roberson has testified:

> I have given invitations in services for the past 54 years.
> In 38½ years at Highland Park Baptist Church in Chatta-
> nooga, I have given an invitation at the close of every
> Sunday morning, Sunday evening, and Wednesday eve-
> ning. We have had a response to every invitation for 38½
> years, with the exception of one service.[7]

A warning must also be sounded. Not to reap the harvest is
to lose the crop. It must be picked when it is ripe; otherwise,

the lament of Jeremiah will apply: "The harvest is past, the summer is ended, and we are not saved" (Jeremiah 8:20).

The biblical support for the issuing of public invitations is substantial. This, of course, does not mean that every convert to Christ has walked a church aisle or responded to an evangelist's appeal. Many people are won to Christ through reading the Bible or personal evangelism. But the biblical record is clear that God not only has used public invitations in the past to bring people to His Son, but also expects preachers to continue issuing such appeals. Pastors and evangelists should boldly call for public decisions for Christ, with complete assurance that the practice can be validated by Scripture.

The Call to New Converts

In the first century, gospel preachers called for new converts to take a public stand for Christ. The apostles expected all true believers to make an open confession of Christ. The Apostle Paul lays down this principle in his epistle to the Romans:

> That if thou shalt confess with thy mouth the Lord Jesus, and shalt believe in thine heart that God hath raised him from the dead, thou shalt be saved. For with the heart man believeth unto righteousness; and with the mouth confession is made unto salvation. For the scripture saith, whosoever believeth on him shall not be ashamed.
>
> (Romans 10:9–11)

A person who believes with his heart "unto righteousness" will willingly make a confession of the fact. The true believer will not be ashamed of his commitment to the Lord.

Confession is an immediate evidence of salvation. Where there is no confession, there is no salvation. William R. Newell says that confession is "the twin sister of faith."[8] There is a direct relationship between faith in the heart and confession with the mouth: "For out of the abundance of the heart the mouth speaketh" (Matthew 12:34). A heart full of faith will express itself in a public witness. A faith that does not produce an open confession is not saving faith. The Apostle Paul affirmed: "We have the same spirit of faith, according as it is written, I believed, and therefore have I spoken; we also believe, and therefore speak" (2 Corinthians 4:13). True faith is always vocalized: "We . . . believe, and therefore speak."

The verb "confess" (Romans 10:9) is translated from the Greek word *homologeō*, and means "to say the same thing" as another, or "to agree with, to assent to a thing." In relation to salvation, the mouth confesses what God's Word says about the subject. This presupposes that the truth has already been embraced by the heart. To confess openly one's total reliance on the Lord Jesus Christ is the initial evidence that he or she is truly indwelt by the Spirit of God (1 John 4:2).

As the believer confesses Christ before others, Christ, the "High Priest of our profession" (*homologeo*—Hebrews 3:1), makes confession of the believer to His Father in heaven: "Whosoever therefore shall confess me before men, him will I confess also before my Father which is in heaven. But whosoever shall deny me before men, him will I also deny before my Father which is in heaven" (Matthew 10:32,33). Further, He said: "Whosoever therefore shall be ashamed of me and of my words in this adulterous and sinful generation, of him also shall the Son of Man be ashamed" (Mark 8:38). John R. W. Stott comments on these passages:

> Now the very fact that Jesus told us not to be ashamed of him shows that he knew we would be tempted to be ashamed; and the fact that he added "in this adulterous and sinful generation" shows that he knew why. He evidently foresaw that his church would be in a minority movement in the world; and it requires courage to side with the few against the many, especially if the few are unpopular.[9]

Like the psalmist who said, "I will speak of thy testimonies also before kings" (Psalms 119:46), every Christian should be unashamed to witness for the Lord.

True faith and outward confession cannot be separated. Martin Luther, the great Reformation leader, explained, "Confession is the principal work of faith: Man denies himself and confesses God and he does this to such an extent that he will deny even his life. . . . Truly, if faith is there he [the believer] cannot hold back; he proves himself, breaks out into good works, confesses and teaches the gospel before the people, and stakes his life on it."[10] That is why the psalmist called out, "Let the redeemed of the Lord say so!" (Psalms 107:2).

The early preachers of the gospel issued two types of invitations. The first called for sinners to repent and exercise faith in the Person and atoning work of Jesus Christ. This often took the form of a public invitation. Once the convert was made, a second type of appeal was issued. The new convert was required, in some manner, to make a public profession of faith in Jesus Christ. This, in essence, sealed his decision; it pointed out the fact that he was a believer. The first-century Christian made such a declaration, knowing full well that, as a result, he would face persecution, alienation from family, friends, and society—possibly even death. His world, controlled by the Roman government, was hostile toward Christianity. To profess Christ openly was to renounce all false gods, including Caesar.

To respond to an invitation to profess Christ publicly, even before enemies of the faith, was evidence that salvation had been wrought in the heart. Conversely, an unwillingness to let it be known that one was a Christian was proof that he was not. While there may have been a few exceptions to this rule, Newell points out that "the early Christians never dreamed of refusing to confess the Lord before men unless they intended to desert Him,"[11] proving themselves to be apostates (1 John 3:19).

A Call to be Baptized

In what manner did the early believers confess their allegiance to Christ? James H. Jauncey believes that the apostolic church considered the ordinance of baptism to be the initial act of public confession.[12] Stott sees a similar connection: "This open confession of Christ cannot be avoided. Paul declared it to be a condition of salvation. . . . The apostle may have been referring to baptism."[13] Faris D. Whitesell, one of the leading authorities on evangelism of a generation ago, has commented:

> Baptism stood for about the same thing in apostolic days as coming forward and making an open declaration of faith does today. Baptism was the public line of demarcation between the old life and the new in New Testament times, and most certainly called for public confession and personal identification with the Christian group.[14]

In essence, water baptism was a public declaration that the sinner had repented of his sins and trusted Christ alone to save him.

Proof that baptism is a strategic part of the evangelistic task is Jesus' inclusion of it in the Great Commission:

> And Jesus came and spake unto them, saying, All power is given unto me in heaven and in earth. Go ye therefore, and teach all nations, *baptizing* them in the name of the Father, and of the Son, and of the Holy Ghost: teaching them to observe all things whatsoever I have commanded you: and, lo, I am with you always, even unto the end of the age.   (Matthew 28:18–20 italics added)

The gospel writer John Mark records the injunction this way: "And he said unto them, Go ye into all the world, and preach the gospel to every creature. He that believeth and is baptized shall be saved; but he that believeth not shall be damned" (Mark 16:15,16). We note that, first, the apostles were commanded to preach and teach the gospel. Second, they were also commanded to baptize. Third, belief was to lead to baptism: a person who believed in his heart was to be baptized in public. God not only requires repentance and faith; He also requires the believer to confess his salvation publicly by submitting to baptism. As long as the Great Commission is in effect, so is the call to be baptized.

When Jesus commissioned His disciples to baptize, He likewise commissioned them to extend a public invitation. The first preachers of the gospel took Jesus' command to baptize seriously. Peter, concluding his sermon on Pentecost, enjoined his listeners:

> Repent and be *baptized* every one of you in the name of Jesus Christ for the remission of sins, and ye shall receive the gift of the Holy Spirit.... Then they that gladly received his word were baptized: and the same day there were added unto them about three thousand souls.
>
> (Acts 2:38,41 italics added)

Philip no doubt issued a similar call for baptism during his evangelistic ministry in Samaria:

> Then Philip went down to the city of Samaria, and preached Christ unto them. And the people with one accord gave heed unto those things which Philip spake. ... When they believed Philip preaching the things concerning the kingdom of God, and the name of Jesus Christ, they were *baptized,* both men and women.
>
> (Acts 8:5,6,12 italics added)

On his return to Jerusalem after the Samaria crusade, Philip was directed by the Spirit to Gaza where he met the Ethiopian eunuch:

> Then Philip opened his mouth, and began at the same
> scripture, and preached unto him Jesus. And as they went
> on their way, they came unto a certain water: and the eu-
> nuch said, See, here is water; what doth hinder me to be
> baptized? And Philip said, If thou believest with all thine
> heart, thou mayest. And he answered and said, I believe
> that Jesus Christ is the Son of God. And he commanded
> the chariot to stand still: and they went down both into the
> water, both Philip and the eunuch; and he baptized him.
>
> (Acts 8:35-38)

The progression is clear. First, the gospel was preached.
Next, faith was produced. Finally, baptism was administered.

An invitation to submit to baptism was given to Saul of
Tarsus shortly after his conversion. This hate-filled persecutor
of the early church was miraculously saved while traveling the
road to Damascus (Acts 9:3-9). The ascended Lord instructed
Saul, blinded by the encounter, to travel to Damascus and go
to the home of Ananias, a believer. There Saul received both
his sight and Ananias' instruction: "Brother Saul, . . . the God
of our fathers hath chosen thee . . . [to] be his witness unto all
men of what thou hast seen and heard. And now why tarriest
thou? Arise, and be *baptized*" (Acts 22:13-16). Luke records
that Saul obeyed the command and submitted to believer's
baptism (Acts 9:18).

The invitation to declare one's faith through baptism was
also extended to the household of Cornelius, the first Gentile
believers. After the Apostle Peter shared the gospel with them,

> the Holy Ghost fell on them which heard the word. . . .
> Then answered Peter, Can any man forbid water that
> these should not be baptized, which have received
> the Holy Ghost as well as we? And he commanded them
> to be *baptized* in the name of the Lord.
>
> (Acts 10:44,46-48 italics added)

The Great Commission, including the call for public baptism, propelled the Apostle Paul through most of the then-known world. On his first missionary journey, Paul traveled to Philippi where he met Lydia, a seller of fine fabrics, "whose heart the Lord opened, that she attended unto the things which were spoken of Paul. And [then] she was *baptized,* and her household" (Acts 16:14,15 italics added). During his stay in Philippi, Paul and his companion Silas were arrested and imprisoned in the local jail. It was here that, following an earthquake, they showed the jailer the way to salvation:

> And they spake unto him the Word of the Lord, and to all that were in his house. And he took them the same hour of the night, and washed their stripes; and was *baptized,* he and all his, straightway. And when he had brought them into his house, he set meat before them, and rejoiced, believing in God with all his house.
>
> (Acts 16:32–34 italics added)

During Paul's trip to Corinth, he "reasoned in the synagogue every sabbath, and persuaded the Jews and the Greeks" (Acts 18:4). One of his converts was a local celebrity: "Crispus, the chief ruler of the synagogue, believed on the Lord with all his house; and many of the Corinthians hearing believed, and were baptized" (Acts 18:8).

The call to public baptism was an important part of the preaching mission of the early church. Those who responded in obedience evidenced their sincerity and faith (Luke 6:46; John 14:15). They were identifying themselves with the crucified and risen Lord (Romans 6:4,5; Colossians 2:12).

That New Testament baptism was for believers only is proof that it differed from the Old Testament practice of circumcision. The latter was conferred upon infant males at eight days of age. To be baptized, on the other hand, the candidate had to be old enough to understand the gospel, repent, and believe.

He also had to be bold enough to present himself for baptism.

For the believer, baptism was a "red badge of courage," showing that he had experienced an inward transformation through the shed blood of the Redeemer. Like a wedding ring, it was an outward sign proclaiming to the world that he had taken on a new responsibility of faithfulness to his Lord.

Whether or not the early preachers extended two separate and distinct appeals—one for sinners to come forward, and another for new converts to be baptized—or whether they somehow combined the two appeals cannot clearly be determined by Scripture. Most likely the heralds of the good news found themselves using both techniques. The record is conclusive that Jesus, as well as the other apostolic preachers, called sinners to publicly step forward as an indication of a contrite and believing heart. This fact was established in the first half of the chapter. The Scripture also affirms that Jesus and His disciples baptized new converts; with Jesus supervising the activities (John 3:26; 4:1,2). This seems to indicate the use of two separate invitations. Peter, on the other hand, only extended a single invitation (Acts 2:38), combining a call for the sinners to repent and be baptized. These two patterns can be traced throughout the four Gospels and the Book of Acts. It may be that the proximity of water was the determining factor as to the nature of the invitation given. If water was nearby a single invitation was issued calling upon sinners to step forward as a sign of repentance and faith, and to present themselves for immediate believer's baptism (Acts 2:38; 8:12; 10:48; 16:15; 16:33; 18:8). The apostles stressed the urgency of believers to respond to baptism. The jailer was baptized at midnight in spite of the lateness of the hour. When water was not available, as in the cases of the Ethiopian eunuch and Saul of Tarsus (Acts 8:36; 9:18), the call for baptism seems to have been separate and distinct from the call to repent and believe.

Why Baptize Today?

Jesus included baptism in the Great Commission, a divine mandate which extends until the end of the age (Matthew 28:20). Unfortunately, most evangelists do not include in their invitational appeals a call for believers to be baptized. This abandonment cannot be justified on scriptural grounds. A clarion call must be sounded to restore baptism to its New Testament place of prominence. Not only does the ordinance proclaim publicly the death, burial, and resurrection of Christ to onlookers, it also serves as an opportunity for the new convert to take a visible stand for the Savior.

When water is available, the pastor or evangelist should conclude his gospel message with an appeal for men to repent and be baptized. The new believer should immediately present himself for baptism. When conditions do not make such an appeal possible, the preacher should give the invitation for sinners to repent and believe by making some other public display of commitment. The new convert should then be told about the importance of believer's baptism, and arrangements should be made for him to be baptized at a future date. The ordinance could be administered by a local pastor at a convenient location.

4

Evangelists and Invitations

Critics of the public invitation claim that its usage can only be traced back to the ministry of Charles G. Finney (1792–1875). Such an accusation is historically incorrect. The first-century preachers of the gospel called on sinners to present themselves publicly as candidates for repentance, faith, and baptism. Similar invitations continued to be given until Constantine, emperor of the Roman Empire, proclaimed Christianity the state religion in 324 A.D. This official union of church and state gave all Roman citizens, regardless of age or spiritual condition, the opportunity to be baptized into the church as members in good standing. In addition, newborn babies were baptized, joining them to the fellowship of the saints. As generations passed, adult baptism was eventually eliminated, since all living Roman citizens had been baptized as infants. With the Roman Empire "Christianized," no longer was the need felt to evangelize and appeal for people to be saved. The public invitation, for the most part, fell by the wayside.

Evangelism continued to prosper outside the Empire among the barbarian tribespeople in Gaul, Spain, and Africa. It also continued within the Empire to a far lesser degree among those who had refused to join the church and were still entrenched in paganism.

In 330 A.D., Constantine moved his capital to Byzantium, located in the Empire's eastern sector, changing the name of the city to Constantinople. This historic move left a vacancy of leadership in the west which the bishop of the church at Rome immediately filled. This particular church claimed pre-eminence over all other established churches throughout the Empire because the Apostle Peter had died and was buried there. He, it was thought, was the cornerstone of the universal church, according to one interpretation of Matthew 16:18. This claim was the seed which eventually grew into the Roman Catholic Church.

From Constantine to the Eighteenth Century

Under Roman Catholicism, sinners were saved by the church, not by the atoning death of Christ. Salvation was obtained by the observance of seven sacraments, and not through a relationship with the living God. Parish priests found it no longer necessary to preach gospel sermons, but replaced them with the reading of prepared homilies handed down from those in authority. Even these were usually read in Latin, a language not understood by the majority of the parishioners. With the rise of Roman Catholicism, history entered the period known as the Dark Ages. For the next several centuries, evangelism was relegated to a place of obscurity until the light of the Reformation shone through in the sixteenth century.

The Reformation was the dawning of a new age. Such leaders as Zwingli, Luther, and Calvin rekindled the spirit of evangelism. Though history does not record any of the reformers issuing the kind of public invitation practiced today, they did conclude their messages by calling sinners to Christ through personal repentance and faith. Those who heeded the appeal were dealt with privately, and later were presented before the congregation to receive communion. This act was the initial public profession of faith for the new convert. It was the first step in restoring the public invitation to its New Testament place of prominence.

Even prior to the Reformation, God was not without a witness. He always had a faithful remnant of believers who refused to obey the decrees and edicts of men at the expense of disobeying God. These selfless servants continued to evangelize by calling upon sinners to repent, believe, and be baptized. Their commitment to the Great Commission often resulted in banishment from the church, exile from the empire, and even death.

Major Pre-Reformation Evangelists

Gregory of Nazianzus (330–389) was a powerful preacher of the gospel during the fourth century. He preached on sin's tragic consequences and the need for repentance and faith. Great throngs, from every stratum of society, packed his local church to hear the Word of God proclaimed. His messages evoked varied responses. Some people broke out into loud, spontaneous applause, while others, convicted of their sins, sat quietly in silent reflection. He claimed many converts to Christ.[1]

The foremost Bible expositor of the period was John Chrysostom of Antioch (347–407). Known as "John, the golden-mouthed," Chrysostom moved his listeners to physical response. One historian writes:

> As he advanced from exposition to illustration, from Scripture principle to practical appeals, his delivery became gradually more rapid, his countenance more animated, his voice more vivid and intense. The people began to hold in their breath. The joints of their loins were loosened. A creeping sensation like that produced by a series of electric waves passed over them. They felt as if drawn forwards toward the pulpit by a sort of magnetic influence. Some of those who were sitting rose from their seats;

others were overcome with a kind of faintness as if the
preacher's mental force were sucking the life out of their
bodies, and by the time the discourse came to an end the
great mass of that spellbound audience could only hold
their heads and give vent to their emotions in tears.[2]

Another important name in early church history is that of
Patrick (c.390–c.461), the first missionary to Ireland. After his
conversion, he felt called to this unevangelized land. Over the
protests of family and friends, he left home to spend more than
a third of a century in vigorous evangelistic work. Describing
Patrick's methods, Robert H. Glover writes:

Everywhere he gathered the people about him in the
open field and preached Christ to them. His burning zeal
and deep sincerity, coupled with a kindly gentleness of
manner, completely won the hearts of the peasants and
nobility alike. He planted hundreds of churches and baptized thousands of converts.[3]

One estimate places converts at 120,000 and new churches at
365 during his missionary endeavors in Ireland.[4]

Boniface (680–754) gave up an opportunity to become the
Bishop of Utrecht in order to take the gospel to the nomadic
tribes of Germany. Upon entering this unevangelized territory,
Boniface was immediately confronted by Thor worshipers.
Like Elijah of old, he challenged their gods and emerged the
victor. During twenty years he baptized over 100,000 converts
for Christ.

The fruitful efforts of Bernard of Clairvaux (1093–1153)
ushered thousands into the kingdom of God. An evangelist
during the Crusades, he issued a public invitation on a regular
basis. Lloyd M. Perry notes, "The basic appeal of Bernard of
Clairvaux was for people to repent of their sins. Often he
would call for a show of hands from those who wished to be
restored to fellowship with God or the church."[5]

(The fact that a call for a show of hands was used as a

method of public invitation during the twelfth century should put to rest the theory that the public invitation first appeared in the ministry of Charles Finney!)

During this same era lived Peter of Bruys (?–c.1131), who strongly spoke out against infant baptism, the veneration of the crucifix, and many other unscriptural practices of the established church. He was a forerunner of the Anabaptist movement, and preached the gospel calling men to repent, believe, and be baptized.

Arnold of Brescia (1100–1155) was another outspoken voice. Like Peter of Bruys, he stood boldly against the Roman Catholic Church and for the gospel and believer's baptism. He was eventually hanged, his body then burned and his ashes emptied into the Tiber River.

Peter Waldo, a wealthy merchant in the city of Lyons, was converted to Christ in 1176. He immediately chose to distribute his wealth to the needy and live out his life as an impoverished preacher of the gospel. Along with his followers, who became known as Waldensians, he promoted an aggressive style of evangelism:

> The method of evangelism adopted by the Waldenses was to go among the people two by two. At first they contacted the populace and gave their message at street corners and in the markets. . . . Their preaching style was very simple and personal. A call to repentance was always a part of their exhortation.[6]

The Waldensians preached scriptural messages in the language of the people. Their converts were immediately baptized. They also repudiated all unscriptural practices of the Roman Catholic churches. As a result, they met with great opposition, persecution, and death. In the midst of oppression they continued to thrive and grow until 1488, when a special campaign was successfully launched against them.

One of the great orators of the thirteenth century was Antony of Padua (1195–1231), whose powerful evangelistic sermons brought revival to entire cities. No church buildings could hold the crowds he drew. T. Harwood Pattison notes that:

> Shops were closed and thoroughfares deserted when he came to any town, and as many as thirty thousand persons would sometimes gather to hear him. His appeals must have been effective, for as he spoke men who came to attack him dropped the dagger and sought his embrace. Women cast off their ornaments and sold them for the benefit of the poor, and old and burdened sinners were brought to immediate confession.[7]

Berthold of Regensberg (c.1210–1272) was an open-air evangelist whose central theme was repentance. Whether or not he ever gave a public invitation, his efforts resulted in many people coming to Christ.

Other evangelists during the Middle Ages included Johann Tauler (c.1300–1361) of Germany; Gerard Groote (1340–1384), whose sermons on repentance and faith were mightily used of God; John Geker (1445–1510) of Kaisersberg, recognized as the greatest of the German preachers; Savonarola (1452–1498), whose messages on repentance and national reform brought revival to Florence; Hugh Latimer (1485–1555), the father of English preaching; and John Wycliffe (c.1329–1384), whose bands of Lollards were the first to hold evangelistic crusades in England during the fourteenth century. The names of scores of others, both famous and obscure, dot the pages of church history books for their faithful contributions in carrying out the Great Commission.

The Anabaptists

Prominent among those Christians who continued faithfully to issue a public invitation were the Anabaptists. Their movement opposed the Church of Rome on the issues of infant baptism, establishment of the priesthood, and the veneration of Mary, among other practices. The Anabaptist group was obedient in calling men to repent of their sins, place their faith in Christ, and present themselves for rebaptism (since their infant baptism was null and void). They met with strong opposition, and many were martyred. Balthasar Hubmaier (1481–1528), the most prominent German Anabaptist of his day, was burned at the stake. His wife was drowned in the Danube River, symbolic of the aversion the established church had to believer's baptism. Prior to his death, Hubmaier had won thousands of converts to Christ.

In Switzerland, Conrad Grebel, father of the Anabaptist movement in that country, was also harshly persecuted. Felix Manz, the scholar of the movement, suffered martyrdom by drowning. George Blaurock, foremost Anabaptist evangelist, was burned at the stake after rebaptizing one thousand new converts in four and one-half years of ministry.

The Anabaptists found themselves the targets of both Catholic and Protestant ire. Although the reformers preached the true gospel and relied on Scripture as their final authority, they opposed the idea of calling people to respond publicly. They felt such a response would be an addition to faith and, therefore, unbiblical. Anabaptists were persecuted for twenty-five years at the hands of the reformers, in large measure because of their stand for believer's baptism. But the Anabaptist movement continued to grow, despite opposition; and by 1573, more than fifty thousand lived in England.

The Puritans

During the Reformation period, a great upheaval took place throughout Christendom. The continental reformers, failing to reform the Roman Catholic Church from within, separated themselves to form what are now called denominations. In England, King Henry VIII broke with Rome because it would not sanction his divorce from Queen Catherine and remarriage to Anne Boleyn. He proclaimed himself head of the Church of England (Anglican), the official state religion. Meanwhile, Puritanism was establishing itself in England as a dynamic evangelical force.

The Puritans were of three persuasions. One faction worked within the Church of England to "purify" it, making little headway. A second class of Puritans advocated reforming the polity of the church along Presbyterian lines, also without success. Though both kept the great doctrines of the Reformation alive, neither group practiced giving a public invitation. (There may have been exceptions. John Bradford was appointed by the King to serve as an itinerant evangelist for the Church of England. He strongly preached repentance and may have issued some kind of public invitation. The Presbyterian Puritans likewise preached repentance, but dealt with the convicted privately. Each pastor would visit his flock once a year to question them sternly regarding their faith.)

The third type of Puritans was known as the Separatists or non-conformists. They broke away from the Church of England and formed their own congregations. In theology they were closer to the Anabaptists than the Anglicans, and most church historians would identify them as spiritual ancestors of the present-day Baptist movements. The Separatists believed that sinners, regardless of their church affiliation, had to repent and believe on Christ to be saved. They also invited converts to confess Christ openly through believer's baptism. The founder of Separatist Puritanism, Thomas Helwys, was driven out of England. In 1609 he migrated to Holland, where he was later martyred for his beliefs.

The most famous of the Separatists, who now called themselves Baptists, was John Bunyan (1628–1688). The renowned author of *Pilgrim's Progress* chose to be imprisoned for twelve years rather than cease preaching the Word of God and the convictions of his conscience, which included a call for public profession of faith.

One Separatist congregation, led by John Robinson and William Bradford, boarded the *Mayflower* and made their historic voyage to America in 1620. They were the Pilgrims, searching for both religious and political liberty in a new land.

The Eighteenth Century

The century that gave the world the Great Awakening also produced some of history's greatest preachers. One was the Jesuit priest Jacques Bridaine (1701–1767), who may have been the first man in modern times to practice effective mass evangelism. He attracted large crowds in France by using processions, music, and large banners to advertise his meetings.[8] His cooperative efforts with local parish priests were most successful. Bridaine issued earnest appeals for people to commit their lives publicly to Christ. The historian Edwin Dargan says that he called for "public avowals of renewed faith or of first confessions of Christ."[9]

America's Great Awakening

In America, Jonathan Edwards (1703–1758), Congregationalist pastor, scholar, and theologian, may have done more through his preaching to bring about the Great Awakening than any other man of his time. He preached on the great themes of the Bible and called sinners to repent and place their faith in the crucified and living Savior. He did not call people to the front of the church, but requested that they meet with him privately for spiritual counsel.[10] Many were converted to Christ through this method. Edwards brought new believers forward to confess Christ for the first time at the communion service. During one eight-week span between communions he wrote:

> I received into one communion about a hundred before one sacrament, and fourscore of them at one time, whose

appearance, when they presented themselves together to
make an open explicit profession of Christianity, was very
affecting to the congregation: I took in nearly sixty before
the next sacrament day.[11]

It is estimated that forty thousand colonists, or twenty-five
percent of the population of America, were won to Christ
through the preaching of such men as Edwards, Gilbert Ten-
nent, Theodore Frelinghuysen, and other leaders of the Great
Awakening.

A significant figure in the Awakening was George Whitefield (1714–1770), who traveled from his native England to
America on several occasions to preach the gospel. He was the
most popular evangelist of his day, gifted with a powerful and
emotional voice that could be heard by crowds of 25,000 at a
time. Whitefield's method of invitation was similar to Edwards, and was the standard procedure during the early eighteenth century. After preaching the gospel and exhorting people to repent and receive Christ, he urged them to make an appointment to see him in private. Often there were so many
"anxious inquirers that he could not find time to eat or
sleep."[12] On one occasion, after preaching in Philadelphia he
recorded in his journal: "Preached at six in the evening from
the Court House stairs to about six thousand people. I find the
number that came on Tuesday to my house [seeking spiritual
instruction] greatly increased and multiplied."[13] Another time
he wrote:

> After preaching, my house was filled with people who
> came in to join in psalms and family prayer. My body was
> weak, but the Lord strengthened me. Many wept most
> bitterly whilst I was praying. Their hearts seemed to be
> loaded with a sense of sin . . . the only preparative for the
> visitation of Jesus Christ.[14]

After preaching a guest sermon for Jonathan Edwards,
Whitefield invited seekers to join him at the pastor's house. His

journal entry reads: "In the evening, I gave a word of exhortation to several who came to Mr. Edwards' house. My body was weak, and my appetite almost gone: but the Lord gave me meat, which the world knows nothing of."[15]

It seems from these accounts that Whitefield made full use of an after meeting to deal with those seeking salvation. Regarding his preaching mission in Kingwood, England, he commented, "Sometimes employed almost morning to night answering those who in distress of soul cried out, 'What must I do to be saved?' "[16]

Another giant of the faith who employed the private consultation method to bring convicted sinners to the Savior was David Brainerd (1718–1747), missionary to the American Indians. Noted for his fervent life of prayer, he wrote in his diary for December 29, 1743:

> After public worship was over, I went to my house, proposing to preach again after a short season of intermission. But soon came in one after another; with tears in their eyes to know "what they should do to be saved." . . . It was an amazing season of power among them, and seemed as if God had "bowed the heavens and came down" . . . and that God was about to convert the whole world.[17]

Wesley and the Methodists

While America was being spiritually awakened, Great Britain was also experiencing tremendous revival. A key figure involved in this move of God was the founder of Methodism, John Wesley (1703–1791). With his brother Charles, he carried the gospel into the hearts of England's common people. Wesley was an innovator when it came to the use of the public invitation. All of his sermons ended with an appeal for listeners to come to Christ. He used four basic methods or forms of the public invitation.[18] First, he employed exhorters or personal workers to be on the lookout for anxious souls. These workers were specially gifted in inviting people to Christ. Spotting a prospect, the exhorter approached him and urged him to make a decision immediately.

A second method was to call upon all seekers to attend the mid-week service where they were to join in the public prayers as an indication of their faith.[19]

A third variation of the public invitation used by Wesley, in common with other early Methodist circuit riders, was to invite the seeker to step forward publicly and present himself for church membership.[20] All the seekers were then formed into local societies for Bible study, prayer, and evangelism. (Over 120,000 aligned themselves with the Methodist movement during Wesley's lifetime.)

Finally, Wesley made use of the mourner's bench or anxious seat.[21] In each meeting house there was reserved a pew where those convicted of their sins and anxious about their soul's salvation could come to receive prayer and spiritual counsel. As the mourner's bench was located at the front of the church, those desiring help needed to make their way forward.

Wesley's use of the mourner's bench predated Finney by more than fifty years. It seems likely that he was the first to practice the use of a mourner's bench. Charles Wesley supposedly uttered, "Oh, that blessed anxious seat"—the first traceable use of the phrase in church history.[22]

The Separatist Baptist movement, despite strong opposition a century earlier, was still a vital force in Europe between 1750 and 1780. According to historian Robert I. Devin, God mightily used the preaching of these brethren to bring many sinners into the Christian faith. Describing a typical service, Devin writes:

> At the close of his sermon, the minister would come down from the pulpit and while [the congregation sang] a suitable hymn would go around among the brethren

shaking hands. The hymn being sung, he would then extend an invitation to such persons as felt themselves to be poor guilty sinners, and were anxiously inquiring the way of salvation, to come forward and kneel down near the stand, or if they preferred to do so, they could kneel at their seats, proffering to unite with them in prayer for their conversion.[23]

The best known of the Separatist Baptists was William Carey (1761–1834), the "father of modern missions." Carey wrote *Enquiry into the Obligations of the Christians to Use Means for the Conversion of the Heathen* after Dr. Rylands, during a ministerial conference, attempted to dissuade Carey from evangelizing the heathen by saying, "Young man, sit down; when God pleases to convert the heathen, He will do it without your aid or mine."[24] Carey rejected this fatalism with the reply, "If it be the duty of all men to believe the gospel . . . then it be the duty of those entrusted with the gospel to endeavor to make it known among all nations."[25] Carey lived the scriptural admonition of the Apostle Paul, "That I might by *all means* save some" (1 Corinthians 9:22).

On both sides of the Atlantic, the public invitation gained gradual acceptance and use. At first, the practical exigencies of the moment dictated technique. In Scotland, the Reverend James Robe, after hearing a Whitefield sermon, became burdened for the souls of his parishioners. For over a year, he preached to them the gospel, urging them to repent and be saved. On May 16, 1742, the Spirit of God moved greatly during his sermon. Robe relates the outcome:

> While pressing all the unregenerate to seek to have Christ formed within them, an extraordinary power of the Divine Spirit accompanied the Word preached. There was great mourning in the congregation, as for an only son. Many cried out, and these not only women, but strong and stout-hearted young men. After the congregation was dis-

missed, an attempt was made to get the distressed into my barn, but their number was so great that this was impossible, and I was obliged to convene them in the kirk. I sung a psalm and prayed with them, but when I assayed to speak to them I could not be heard, so great were their bitter cries, groans, and the voice of their weeping. After this I requested that they might come into my closet one by one. I sent for the Rev. John Oughterson, minister of Cumberland, who immediately came to assist me in dealing with the distressed.[26]

Local church records in America document numerous instances of pastors calling seekers forward—whether planned or not—for prayer and counsel. One such improvised call took place in October, 1741 at the Reverend Eleazer Wheelock's church in Lebanon, Connecticut. The church record indicates that the Reverend Mr. Wheelock's sermon was interrupted numerous times with sobs from the congregation. The record continues: "Wherefore being able to finish his sermon, with great apparent serenity and calmness of soul—he called to the distressed to gather in the seats below so he could more conveniently converse with them."[27]

In 1785 in Tennessee, the Reverend John Taylor felt led to call inquirers to the front of his church. He records the incident: "When I stopped speaking, two men and their wives . . . rose up, and with trembling, came forward, and asked me to pray for them. . . . The thing being so new to the people, it spread a heavenly blaze through the assembly."[28]

By the close of the century, the "new thing" was taking root. Well-known Methodist evangelist Lorenzo Dow had begun using a progressive invitation. He first would ask those who wanted their souls prayed for to so signify by standing to their feet. Then he invited all seekers immediately to move to the front for prayer.[29]

The first recorded use of the altar in connection with a public invitation occurred in 1799. At a Methodist camp meeting at Red River, Kentucky, an altar was erected in front of the pulpit "designed as a place for penitents, where they might be collected together for prayer and instruction."[30] The altar was so effective a means of bringing sinners into a saving knowledge of Christ that many Methodist churches installed one as a permanent fixture.[31] The altar's value was threefold. It gave those needing spiritual help an opportunity to indicate their need by going forward. The altar was also a symbol that one must be willing to take a public stand for Christ. Finally, it was tangible proof of the seeker's willingness to take decisive action in order to be saved.

The Nineteenth Century

The nineteenth century saw the Second Great Awakening and the emergence of Charles Grandison Finney (1792–1875). Finney, whose writings on revival are still read today, was a successful trial lawyer before his conversion to Christ. His legal mind proved helpful in developing convincing sermons designed to win a verdict for Christ. As an evangelist, Finney was very successful. His low-key, conversational method of preaching made each member of the audience feel that Finney was speaking directly to him.

Finney experimented with many types of public invitations. Until 1822 he asked those anxious about their souls to stand at their seats as a sign of a repentant heart.[32] He later combined this method with an invitation for the convicted to move forward to the mourner's bench, where they could be instructed, receive prayer, and be led to Christ. It was during his highly acclaimed Rochester, New York crusade (1830) that Finney began to make exclusive use of the mourner's bench. Though not the first to employ this method, Finney was certainly the one who popularized its use. Many local pastors cooperating in the evangelistic campaign began using the mourner's bench during their regular Sunday and midweek services.

The mourner's bench was not an end in itself. After the close of a meeting, Finney would gather the penitents together in a separate room or building where he and fellow pastors could answer their questions, correct their erroneous doctrines, and lead them to a saving knowledge of Jesus Christ. This room was called the "inquiry room."

In his later ministry, Finney abandoned use of the anxious seat altogether and began simply to invite seekers to come forward into the aisles and kneel down at the front of the auditorium.[33]

Asahel Nettleton (1783–1844), a contemporary of Finney, was the first American-born evangelist. He used the inquiry room or anxious meeting, as it was often called, "for those who felt they were ready for such an adventure."[34] C. E. Autrey explains Nettleton's reasoning:

> The inquiry room gave him a chance to separate those under conviction from the rest of the congregation in order to properly instruct them. In the inquiry room individuals could speak with others without the excitement and pressure of the crowd.[35]

William Booth (1829–1912) frequently used a public invitation. It is no wonder he did, since he was converted under such a method! Fred Barlow writes:

> He began attending Broad Street Wesleyan Chapel and once, after hearing a disturbing discourse on "A Soul Dies Every Minute," and reflecting on his sins, young William Booth "publicly repented and made the surrender of his soul to God."[36]

Booth later became a Methodist pastor before resigning to take the gospel to down-and-outers under the banner of The

Salvation Army. It was in Cornwall, England that Booth "introduced the altar bench in his meetings, and it has always been a regular feature in Salvation Army services since."[37]

The man who epitomizes the office of pastor-evangelist in modern church history is Charles Haddon Spurgeon (1834–1892). Roland Q. Leavell characterizes his sermons as "textual and expository, Calvinistic in doctrine, and unfailingly evangelistic in appeal. Every sermon led to Christ."[38] Dr. I. D. E. Thomas, one of the foremost authorities on Puritanism, wrote that Spurgeon "beautifully combines Puritan preaching with an evangelistic invitation, using the enquiry room."[39] According to Eric Hayden, the architecture of the Metropolitan Tabernacle in London did not lend itself to hundreds coming forward, so Spurgeon did the next best thing: he "would often request enquirers to go below to one of the basement lecture halls to be counseled by his elders."[40] At other times, he would call for the anxious to remain in their seats until the rest of the congregation left the building. Then their spiritual needs were met. Spurgeon also used his elders as exhorters constantly "on watch for souls."

When asked to comment on Dwight L. Moody's method of inviting people to stand to be saved, Spurgeon remarked, "I believe that it is a great help in bringing people to a decision when Mr. Moody asks those to stand who wish to be prayed for. Anything that tends to separate you from the ungodly around you is good for you."[41]

Absalom B. Earle (1812–1895), a Baptist evangelist used of God in the nineteenth century, "urged convicted sinners to come forward either to the 'anxious benches,' or to an inquiry room"[42] at the conclusion of his messages. He was the first evangelist to make use of a commitment card:[43]

> Each person who came forward signed a card to indicate his pledge to live a Christian life and to show a church preference. This portion of the card was retained

by the personal worker, so some type of follow-up could be worked out. Another portion of the card was given to the new Christian as a guide for Christian living.[44]

The great evangelist of love, Dwight L. Moody (1837–1899), brought the nineteenth century to a close. A converted shoe store clerk with only a fourth-grade education, Moody was able to reach the man on the street with the gospel. He employed a two-step, progressive invitation. He first urged all who wanted to be saved to stand.[45] (Sometimes, they were requested to stand and indicate their desire to receive Christ by saying, "I will.") Those standing were then invited into the inquiry room for counsel. Moody would come down from the pulpit, pass through the aisles with outstretched hands, and motion for the people to continue rising and follow him into the inquiry room. Only inquirers and Moody-trained counselors were admitted into the room. Each counselor was then matched with an inquirer. After the inquirer's name, address and church were secured, counseling began.

One momentous occasion in Dwight L. Moody's ministry was witnessing his mother publicly receive Christ through his preaching. Closing a message at the old Congregational Church in Northfield, Illinois, in 1876, Moody gave a passionate plea for sinners to be saved:

> His mother sat near the front, and was one of the first to rise for prayer. When he saw her, tears of joy filled his eyes, his voice choked, and turning to B. F. Jacobs, of Chicago . . . he asked him to pray, saying,
> *"That's my mother!"*[46]

What made Moody's evangelistic efforts, and his invitation in particular, so effective? One writer, analyzing Moody's sermon "The Blood," helps supply the answer:

> The most striking thing about "The Blood" was how it was organized to compel the hearers to act, not just listen;

they had either to agree to do what Moody was asking them to do, or deliberately refuse to do it. This was the essential structure of *all* his revival sermons.[47]

The last sermon Moody ever preached contained the following invitation. Based on Luke 14:16–24, the parable of the great feast, it illustrates how effectively he was able to call men to Christ:

> Suppose we should write out tonight this excuse, how would it sound? "To the King of Heaven: While sitting in Convention Hall, Kansas City, Mo., November 16, 1899, I received a very pressing invitation from one of your servants to be present at the marriage supper of your only begotten Son. I pray Thee have me excused."
>
> Would you sign that, young man? Would you, mother? Would you come up to the reporter's table, take a pen and put your name down to such an excuse? You would say, "Let my right hand forget its cunning, and my tongue cleave to the roof of my mouth, before I sign that." I doubt if there is one here who would sign it. Will you, then, pay no attention to God's invitation? I beg of you, do not make light of it. It is a loving God inviting you to a feast, and God is not to be mocked. Go play with forked lightning, go trifle with pestilence and disease, but trifle not with God.
>
> Just let me write out another answer. "To the King of Heaven: While sitting in Convention Hall . . . I received a pressing invitation from one of your messengers to be present at the marriage supper of your only begotten Son. I hasten to reply. By the grace of God I will be present."
>
> Who will sign that? Is there one here who will put his name to it? Is there no one who will say, "By God's grace I will accept the invitation now"? May God bring you to a decision now. If you would ever see the kingdom of God, you must decide this question one way or the other. What will you do with the invitation? I bring it to you in the name of my Master; will you accept or reject it? Be wise

tonight, and accept the invitation. Make up your mind that you will not go away till the question of eternity is settled.[48]

The Twentieth Century

Following Moody's death, Sam Jones (1847–1906) became the most popular evangelist in America. A trial lawyer whose career was ruined by alcoholism, Jones was saved during a revival service conducted by his grandfather. Three verses of the invitation hymn had been sung before Jones gathered enough courage to step forward and give his life to Christ. He dated his conversion from that day.

Sam Jones became a circuit-riding Methodist preacher, fighting sin, alcohol, and the devil. Labeled "the Moody of the South," he would often hold three meetings a day to crowds exceeding five thousand. His method of public invitation varied. Sometimes he asked those convicted to come forward. On other occasions, he would first ask them to stand or raise their hands. Those who responded were then counseled in the front seats of the church or auditorium. A typical Jones invitation went like this:

> God have mercy on men who will let the last chance of being saved pass away and then go into eternity unprepared. Will you risk it? Will you risk it? How many men sitting before me, or anywhere in this church tonight, who are not religious, who are not professors of religion, young men who are not religious, fathers who are not religious, how many of you will stand up before God and man and say, "I don't want to do without religion; I want to be a Christian here and live with Christians here on earth and with them forever hereafter"? How many of you will stand up tonight and say, "God being my judge, I do not want to die a sinner. I want to be a Christian; I want to be saved from sin"? Have you interest enough in your soul to stand

up and say: "I want the prayers of all who pray. I want to be saved from my sins"? Will you stand up—every person who wants to be a Christian and shun the death that never, never dies—will you stand up? Do not be ashamed or afraid.[49]

And now I will say to the congregation, we are going to have an after service, and all of you that want to retire do so. Every one of you who are not Christians who stood up, stay with us and come to the front. All who did not stand up, and are Christians, come to the front, and may God tonight give us one hundred souls for Christ. Oh, friend, do not leave here if you are not a Christian! I trust tonight one hundred or more honest penitents will come and take their seats in front here and tell me, "I want to know God."[50]

How effective was Sam Jones' invitation? Most of his evangelistic campaigns averaged two thousand converts. By the end of his illustrative career, he had spoken to more than twenty-five million people, with over half a million responding to the public invitation.

Like Jones, Reuben A. Torrey (1856–1928) had his most productive years of ministry during the early 1900s. In three and one half years, from 1901 to 1905, Torrey won over a hundred thousand people to Christ at home and abroad. Torrey was a great Bible teacher, preaching on the fundamental doctrines of the Christian faith. He had a unique ability to arrange his sermons in such a manner that they built up to a dramatic climax.

Those who responded to his appeal to receive Christ were asked to stand and say, "I will." Torrey would acknowledge each response, whenever possible, by replying, "God bless you." All converts standing were then asked to repeat, after Torrey, the following prayer of confession: "I have taken Jesus as my Savior, my Lord, and my King." Next, an invitation was extended for them to come forward and occupy several rows of empty seats where they would receive additional prayer and counsel from a trained worker. While these inquirers were being counseled, personal workers roamed through the audience pleading earnestly with those who had resisted Torrey's original appeal. This lasted for five minutes. Many additional converts were made through this process. It was then Torrey's turn to address all the new converts who had gathered at the front.[51]

Dr. A. C. Dixon (1854–1925), an American pastor-evangelist from North Carolina, was called in 1911 to fill the pulpit at the Metropolitan Tabernacle in London, England. To fill the shoes of the late Charles Haddon Spurgeon and his successors was a big task. Dixon received much criticism when he began calling people "to come forward and accept Christ."[52] The British were not accustomed to such a bold and direct invitation. Dixon held his ground by saying that he believed in "striking while the iron was hot." He felt that waiting for people to gather for an after meeting would allow them time to equivocate.

One of the most tender-hearted evangelists ever used by God was Rodney "Gipsy" Smith (1860–1947). Born a natural gypsy, Rodney Smith was saved at the age of sixteen in a little Methodist chapel in Cambridge, England. He immediately began to do evangelistic work with The Salvation Army. He later joined the Methodist Church as an evangelist and made several trips to America. Thousands responded to his call to receive Jesus Christ publicly as Lord and Savior.

During World War I, Gipsy Smith ministered to the British troops in France. The compassion he used in drawing men to Christ could manifest itself even in the heat of battle:

> I was talking behind the lines to some of the boys. Every boy in front of me was going up to the trenches that night. There were five or six hundred of them. It wasn't easy to talk. All I said was accompanied by the roar of guns, the crack of rifles, and the rattle of machine guns, and once in

a while our faces were lit up by the flashes. I looked at those boys. I couldn't preach to them in any ordinary way. I knew, and they knew, that for many it was the last service for some on earth.

I said, "Boys, you are going up to the trenches. Anything may happen there. I wish I could go with you. God knows I do. I would if they would let me, and if any of you fell, I would like to hold your hand and say something to you for your mother, for wife, and for lover, and for your little child. I'd like to be the link between you and home just that moment—God's messenger for you. They won't let me go; but there is Somebody who will go with you. You know who that is?" You should have heard the boys all over that hut whisper, "Yes, sir, Jesus."

"Well," I said, "I want every man that is anxious to take Jesus with him into the trenches to stand." Instantly and quietly every man stood.[53]

Under normal circumstances, Gipsy Smith invited his hearers to come forward to receive Christ, but flexible evangelist that he was, he could adjust his method when the situation warranted it.

A history of the invitation would be incomplete without Billy Sunday (1862–1935), the "baseball evangelist," who preached to more than one hundred million people in his lifetime and witnessed one million make public professions of faith in Christ.[54] In his 1915 Philadelphia campaign alone, over forty thousand "hit the sawdust trail."[55]

In the early years of his ministry, Sunday used a progressive invitation. He first made an appeal for the convicted to come forward. Without any help from the choir or coaxing from the musicians, people began to come. Sunday waited quietly. When the flow forward slowed down, personal workers were sent into the audience to exhort others to come. Then Sunday would signal the choir. Under the direction of Homer Rodeheaver, a musical invitation would begin. Scores joined the throngs at the front. After addressing the new converts, Billy turned them over to counselors to receive further instruction.

In later years, Sunday simply invited sinners to come forward to receive Christ. Usually a vocalist sang an invitational hymn, accompanied by the choir. Exhorters were no longer used. A typical Sunday invitation came right to the point:

> You know that God has spoken to you. You know that without Christ you are lost, and that with Him you are saved ... and now without another word from me, and before anyone can have a chance to say any thing to you, how many of you will settle the great question without delay of another minute, by coming forward to take me by the hand, and by doing so confess and accept Jesus Christ as your personal Savior? Who will come?[56]

Billy Sunday shook hands with eighty-four converts a minute.[57] Two lines would form on each side of the pulpit. Standing in the middle, he could shake hands with two people at a time, one with each hand.

Sawdust was used in all Billy Sunday meetings beginning in 1910 with the Bellingham, Washington campaign.[58] The expression "hitting the sawdust trail" originated in Bellingham, a lumbering community. Sunday learned that the woodsmen were often required to penetrate and work in thick forests. So as not to get lost, they carried with them several bags of sawdust which they sprinkled on the ground to form a trail along the way. When it was time to return home, they simply followed the sawdust trail to safety. Sunday spiritualized the concept and adapted it to his meetings. He called sinners to follow the sawdust trail to the front of the tabernacle and thus find their way home to Christ.[59]

The sawdust also met a practical need. It served to dull the sound of the hundreds of feet that were coming to the front.[60]

The name Jack Van Impe (1931–   ) is known to fundamental Christians around the world. He is the only preacher of this generation who has been able to unite fundamentalist churches in mass evangelism.[61] By 1973, over 125,000 people responded to the gospel invitation to receive Christ as Savior in Jack Van Impe crusades. An additional half-million made public rededications.

Early in his ministry, Van Impe established a policy concerning the use of the public invitation. His biographer writes:

> He knew there were gimmicks and tricks, used by many preachers, designed to get as many people as possible to come forward. Some of these methods bordered on dishonesty and his heart wouldn't allow him to employ them. He concluded that his invitation to the lost and backslidden would be straightforward and easy to understand, with no traps for his listeners. He wanted decisions and public professions as much as anyone, but was not willing to use carnal means to get them. Convinced that the real results of a meeting are recorded in heaven, he has held to an honest and open invitation and the Lord has rewarded him with many souls. Pastors across the country have learned they can trust him to handle this sensitive part of a meeting with reverence and good taste.[62]

Evangelist Luis Palau (1934–   ) is known as "the Billy Graham of Latin America."[63] Considered the foremost evangelist in the Spanish-speaking world today, Palau originally had great difficulty in accepting any type of public invitation. His strong Plymouth Brethren background told him that public invitations spoke only to man's emotions, not his heart and soul. Palau was able finally to overcome his skepticism when, after much prayer, God convinced him the practice was valid. He tells of the first time he called men to profess Christ publicly:

> During my prayer I got the definite urge to give an invitation that night. It was so strong that I felt I would be sinning to disobey it. Then I just hoped for a crowd.

About seventy-five townspeople packed the place. I could hardly wait to preach, especially knowing that I would be giving the first bona fide public invitation of my life. Many of the people appeared anxious to receive Christ at the street meeting, and I saw a few of them there that night.

I preached on John 10:28,29 (NAS): "I give eternal life to them, and they shall never perish; and no one shall snatch them out of My hand. My Father, who has given them to Me, is greater than all; and no one is able to snatch them out of the Father's hand."

It's a powerful passage of assurance that really speaks for itself. As I neared the end I felt free to invite people to receive Christ. I gave the invitation that night the same way I have now done it for years. I asked them to bow their heads and pray along with me silently if they wanted to receive Christ.

I prayed the simple prayer of confession, seeking forgiveness and inviting Christ into the heart. Then I asked those who prayed with me to raise their hands to signify their decision. I counted thirty-five hands and nearly panicked.[64]

Luis Palau's invitation today differs little from the first one he ever extended. After preaching his message, he asks everyone to bow his head. Those who desire to receive Christ are asked to repeat silently a sinner's prayer of repentance and faith. As the choir sings, those who offered the prayer are asked to come to the front of the platform as an initial act of public confession before their peers.[65] Palau does not see this invitation for people to come forward as a call for salvation. They were saved the moment they sincerely called upon the Lord. He invites the new converts to *proclaim* their salvation publicly by stepping to the front of the auditorium or arena.

The late Lewis Sperry Chafer, founder of Dallas Theological Seminary, opposed public invitations for salvation. He did believe, however, that invitations for public confessions made by *new converts* were valid:

> The real value of public methods may be secured and many evils avoided if, after explaining the way of life and during a season of silent prayer, the unsaved are asked to accept Christ by a conscious act of the will, directed in definite silent prayer to God. Such a decision may then be greatly strengthened by an immediate public confession of Christ. The vital difference in question is, however, that such are then confessing that they have believed on Christ, rather than making a confession in order that they may be saved. After such an appeal, an opportunity should be made for personal conversation with any who believe they have accepted Christ by faith, or any others who may have honest difficulties. In this conversation the individual's exact understanding of the step may be ascertained and his faith strengthened. Such conversations may be secured early in an after meeting, or by offering some attractive literature suited to beginners in the Christian life. When it is clear that an intelligent decision has been made, constant confession of Christ as personal Savior should be urged along with the other duties and privileges of the new life.[66]

Many other choice servants of Christ have contributed through the years to the development of the public invitation, among them B. Fay Mills, J. Wilbur Chapman, William B. Riley, Mordecai Ham, Paul Rader, Bob Jones, Sr., John R. Rice, Hyman Appelman, W. A. Criswell, Grady Wilson, and Leighton Ford. Due largely to their combined efforts, the twentieth century has witnessed the public invitation restored to its New Testament place of prominence. As Jesus called men to repent and believe in public fashion, so the modern-day evangelist follows in the steps of his Master by issuing the invitation.

5

Billy Graham's Use of the Public Invitation

William Franklin Graham, Jr., (1918–), better known to millions simply as "Billy," has preached the gospel to more people than any man in history. Like other great evangelists before him, he has been totally committed to the use of the public invitation. Every one of his gospel messages is followed by an appeal for listeners to respond in some visible manner, thereby indicating their desire to repent and believe on Jesus Christ for salvation.

Graham himself was saved under such circumstances. In November 1934, Mordecai Ham, at the invitation of the local Christian Business Men's Committee (CBMC), conducted his now-famous Charlotte, North Carolina crusade. A temporary tabernacle was erected on Pecan Avenue to accommodate five thousand people. Sawdust and wood shavings covered the floor. Sixteen-year-old Billy Graham attended several of the nightly meetings until he could no longer resist the drawing power of the Holy Spirit. As Ham called upon sinners to come forward and repent, Billy along with his friend Grady Wilson, responded. Years later he would write: "When the invitation was given, I made my way to the front with the others. I gave my hand to the preacher (Mordecai Ham) and my heart to the

Savior. Immediately joy, peace, and assurance flooded my soul."[1]

Billy Graham does not believe that merely making a public profession is a guarantee of personal salvation. Without the inward working of the Holy Spirit, an outward profession is empty and meaningless. As Graham says, "It was not just the technique of walking forward in a Southern revival meeting. It was Christ. I was conscious of Him."[2]

Graham Begins Using the Public Invitation

After graduating from high school, Billy Graham enrolled in Bob Jones University before transferring in mid-year to Florida Bible Institute (now Trinity Bible College). It was here that he was called by God to preach and learned how to give a public invitation.

On one occasion, he was invited by the school dean to attend the evening service of a small Baptist church in Palatka, Florida. Without warning he was called upon to preach. Nervously, he delivered an eight-minute evangelistic message and closed by calling upon listeners who wanted to be saved to raise their hands.[3] There were three or four responses. Billy then called upon the respondents to come forward. All did except one—a huge woodsman. When Billy stepped from the pulpit and confronted the brute of a man for not moving forward, he got an unexpected, embarrassing retort: "You don't need to think because you go to that school down there that you know everything."[4] This was an experience that Billy would never forget.

As a student at Florida Bible Institute, Graham often served as a supply pastor, filling pulpits for vacationing or ill pastors. The first time he was officially invited to preach, he and a fellow student, who served as song leader, were disappointed that the congregation seemed so unresponsive. The two boys, therefore, spent all afternoon praying that God would move mightily in the evening service. They were astonished at the results.

> Billy thought his sermon indifferent, but when he gave the invitation, thirty-two young men and women came forward.... The superintendent of the Sunday School, Mr. Baird, remarked afterward, "There's a young man who is going to be known around the world."
>
> On the way back to Tampa ... Billy (said), "I've learned my greatest lesson. It is not by power or might or any fancy sermon; it's wholly and completely the work of the Holy Spirit."[5]

After completing his course of study at Florida Bible Institute, Billy enrolled in Wheaton College in Illinois where he completed the requirements for a Bachelor's degree in anthropology. After graduation, he accepted a call to pastor the First Baptist Church in Western Springs, Illinois. A biographer, Stanley High, comments about Graham's pastorate:

> Billy Graham, even while a pastor, was more evangelist. He preached every Sunday morning and every Sunday evening as though each service were a revival. In a sense, each service was. He never failed to give a call for "decisions for Christ"; almost always there was someone or several who came forward.[6]

Within a very short time it became clear to everyone that Billy Graham's gift lay in the area of evangelism, not the pastorate. In 1945 he joined the fledgling Youth For Christ organization as its vice president and first fulltime evangelist. One of his first YFC evangelistic meetings was held in Chicago's Orchestra Hall. Over three thousand people were in attendance—at the time, the largest audience he had ever addressed. He accompanied his sermon with a call for sinners to come forward and give their lives to Christ. Over forty persons responded to the public invitation.[7]

The ministry of Billy Graham as an evangelist was officially underway. He would eventually resign his post with Youth For Christ to begin his own evangelistic association.

The Evolution of the Graham Invitational Style

Billy Graham originally issued a progressive style invitation. His call for sinners to repent and believe included three essential elements.[8] First, he asked that all heads be bowed. Next, those who wished to repent and believe were to raise their hands. Finally, he called for all who had raised their hands to leave their seats and come forward, while those who remained seated kept their heads bowed in prayer. This writer has personally reviewed several films of the early Billy Graham crusades. In every film which included footage on the invitation, the progressive method was used.

In the film "Mid-Century Crusade," covering the 1950 Portland, Oregon meetings, Graham can be seen asking people to bow their heads for prayer. At this point a section of the invitation is spliced out of the film. During this interval of time Graham has apparently asked for a show of hands of those who want to be saved. The film picks up with Billy Graham exhorting, "You come, *you who lifted your hands,* you come." As the choir sings "Just As I Am," the evangelist continues to exhort:

> That's it, you come! Outside. Inside. You come, that's it. Come, come. As everyone in this place prays for you, you come. Hundreds of you. Give your heart to Christ tonight. Many are coming. You come. Sing it again softly as others come. That's it, come on. Many are coming. You come. God bless you. Come on.[9]

All who responded were then ushered into an adjacent prayer tent or room, where each inquirer was counseled by a personal worker.

Graham's official biographer, John Pollock, records the use of the progressive invitation during the 1950 Columbia, South Carolina Crusade. After preaching on Noah and the flood,

> Billy cried suddenly, "I wonder how many people there
> are here today who will say, 'Right where I sit I want Jesus
> to come into my heart. I want to make sure right now'?"
> Hundreds of hands went up. Billy stopped abruptly. He
> gave the invitation to come forward. A moment later . . .
> the choir began to sing.[10]

Billy Graham continued to use the progressive invitation
successfully into the mid-1950s. (It was the method that he had
used in his historic 1949 "Christ for Greater Los Angeles"
Crusade, closing his sermons with prayer before issuing a call
for hands and a public response.)[11] Attempting to explain the
reason for Graham's success in those early years, David Poling
states, "Billy had a clarity and freshness that urged his listeners
to get up out of their seats and come forward."[12]

By the 1957 New York City Crusade, Graham had dropped
his request for people to raise their hands. One message entitled "The Sermon on the Mount" concluded with these words:
"Get up out of your seat. While our heads are bowed, you
come. Quickly! From all over this building, you come."[13]

Following his sermon, "Why God Gave the Law," delivered
in Melbourne, Australia in 1959, Billy closed with the exhortation: "While our heads are bowed and eyes are closed, I am
going to ask you to come. No one looking around. You come
as an indication of giving your life to Christ."[14] Graham's invitation had evolved into a two-step approach: prayer and
public response. No longer did he ask for a show of hands.

The two-step method was still being used in 1963. Graham
closed his sermon, "Lost Frontier," during the Greater Southern California Crusade by appealing to his listeners: "Get up
out of your seat and say by coming, 'I receive Christ.' With
every head bowed and no one moving around, you come."[15]

By the middle of the 1960s, Billy was issuing a simple one-
step invitation: exhorting listeners simply to leave their seats
and make their way to the front of the platform. He stopped

insisting that all heads be bowed as people came forward. Whenever it was physically impossible for people to move forward, Billy would ask his hearers to either stand or raise their hands as a sign of repentance and belief.[16] Today, whatever public response he calls for, he never issues more than a one-step invitation.

After extending the invitation, Graham usually steps back from the podium to wait for the response:

> He stands in one place behind the pulpit, his arms folded, his head slightly bowed, his chin cupped in one hand. He does not plead or cajole or argue or call upon his associates to witness to the numbers coming, as he once did.[17]

Very rarely as the choir sings "Just As I Am" does Billy interject an additional appeal for people to come forward. He patiently waits for the flow of people to subside. He then addresses the assembled inquirers on the basics of successful Christian living. This usually takes less than five minutes. Each inquirer is then paired off with a counselor who offers further instruction and helpful Christian literature and materials.

How a Billy Graham Invitation Works

Billy Graham does not prepare his invitations; he extends them extemporaneously.[18] This does not mean they are given haphazardly, or lack form and design. All of Graham's invitations are very structured and contain certain essential facts which the evangelist wishes to convey to his listeners. Over the years a Graham-style invitation has emerged, one so uniquely his own that it cannot successfully be duplicated by others. Graham's invitation has taken on his personality. He has given it birth; it is a part of him. At invitation time, Billy knows exactly what he wants to say and do.

Preparing Hearts for the Invitation

Billy Graham preaches for a verdict. He calls men to make a decision which will affect the destiny of their souls. Realizing that both preacher and listener bear responsibility before God, Billy is constantly calling them to come to Christ during his sermon. He wants to make certain his hearers not only understand the gospel message, but that they clearly comprehend what response is required of them. Billy does not issue one lone invitation at the conclusion of his message, but sprinkles several preliminary invitations throughout.

Six of his ten published sermons from the 1969 New York Crusade begin with an invitation.[19] His opening remarks to the sermon, "The Other Death," are typical of the majority of his messages:

> I'm going to ask that we bow our heads in prayer. Every head bowed and every eye closed in prayer. On this Sunday evening there are hundreds of people in this auditorium who need to make the commitment to Christ that Jerome Hines made fifteen years ago. You, too, have a sense of guilt and frustration and confusion in your life. The problems are just too great for you to cope with. Real hangups. You need help. There's an uncertainty about death. You're not sure where you're going if you died. You can find an answer tonight right here by making your commitment to Jesus Christ who died on the cross for you.
>
> Our Father and our God, we pray that Thy Holy Spirit will speak to our hearts tonight and convince us of sin and righteousness and judgment and point us to the Lamb of God that taketh away the sin of the world. For we ask it in His name. Amen.[20]

During the 1981 Greater Baltimore Crusade, Graham began five of his eight evangelistic sermons with an appeal for sinners to receive Christ.

Billy Graham's opening and preliminary invitations are part of his evangelistic style. He consciously issues these initial appeals in an effort to prepare the people for the final call. Writing on the importance of the invitation, Graham states:

> I begin the invitation as I am introducing my message. In any given audience there are those people whose heart God has prepared. I like to mention this fact as I start speaking and have special prayer for those who will be affected by the gospel. Then, often during the message, before the final invitation, I make an appeal for audience response to start individuals thinking about personal commitment.[21]

The Transition

Billy Graham makes a smooth and rapid transition from the body of his sermon into the final invitation. It is so smooth, in fact, that it goes virtually unnoticed. One of Graham's biographers expressed his surprise at how quickly the evangelist had moved into the invitation without any visible break in continuity.[22]

What is the secret of this apparent effortlessness? In most of his sermons, Graham begins his invitation with a key transitional question. In a message entitled "Fear," for example, Billy closes the body of his sermon with these words:

> The Bible declares that for those in Christ there is no judgment. The Bible declares that the sting of death is gone for those who are in Christ. Your fears are banished. Your frustrations quieted. Your worries can flee if today you give your heart and life to Jesus Christ. Right where you are now you can say "Yes" to Christ. You say, "But Billy, what do I have to do?"[23]

The key question enables Graham to move smoothly into his invitation. In the sermon "Sin," he makes the transition in similar fashion:

And I want to tell you that Jesus Christ will march out of this building with you tonight to answer your prayers, to forgive your sins, to make you a new person, if you will open your heart and life and let him in.

You say, "Well, Billy, what do I have to do?"[24]

The pattern is repeated in nearly all of Graham's sermons. The main part of his sermon on "The Other Death" concludes: "If there's a doubt in your heart tonight that you're ready to meet God, I hope you'll receive Christ as your Savior. You say, 'Well, Billy, what do I have to do?' "[25]

The context may vary, but the key phrase is a constant. His "Prodigal Son" sermon ended on this note: "What Christ has done for Jim Vaus, He can do for you tonight if you put your faith and confidence in Him. I am going to ask you to do it tonight. You ask, 'What do I have to do, Billy?' "[26]

In the sermon "Will God Spare America?", Graham closed with the following exhortation:

He's giving you one more chance to say "Yes" to Jesus Christ. And if you don't, the Scripture teaches that God will spare not—God will spare not, and it means hell, the lake of fiery brimstone, for everyone who rejects Jesus Christ.

You say, "Well, Billy, what do I have to do?"[27]

Graham once ended a sermon on the topic of Christ's second coming with, "But you say, 'Billy, what do I have to do to be ready?' "[28]

The transitional question, "What must I do?" simply verbalizes for Graham's hearers a query that silently resides within their hearts. Three times in the New Testament, at the conclusion of a gospel message, the listeners cried out, "What must I do?" (Luke 3:10, Acts 2:37; 16:30). Every sermon should raise this vital question in the hearts and minds of the congregation; and every invitation should supply an appropriate answer (Luke 3:11; Acts 2:38, 16:31). Billy Graham takes this principle one step further. He makes sure the question is raised in the heart by audibly expressing it. He also uses this question as a means of moving directly into his final invitation.

Answering the Query

Having asked the transitional question on behalf of his audience, Billy Graham then proceeds to answer it. His answer always includes three points. First, man must repent of his sins. Second, he must place his faith in the crucified and risen Lord Jesus Christ alone for salvation. Finally, he must be committed to live a life in obedience to Christ. This includes confessing Christ publicly. Each of these points is explained fully. Often Graham will give illustrations to clarify the meaning of repentance, faith, and obedience. He wants to make certain all of his hearers have a grasp on the truth. No one must be left outside the kingdom due to a lack of understanding.

Graham's presentation is very logical and well structured. Rarely, if ever, does he use emotion as a means to win people to Christ. In the instruction phase of his invitation, Billy Graham the evangelist becomes Billy Graham the teacher. He offers a straightforward answer to the question, "What must I do to be saved?"

The Call for Public Commitment

After explaining what God expects from each person in light of the gospel, Billy Graham issues his formal public invitation:

> I'm going to ask you to make that decision. I'm going to ask you to get up out of your seats, all over this vast arena, and come and stand in front of this platform and stand here quietly. And after you've all come I'm going to say a word to you and have a prayer with you. Then a counselor will say a word to you and you can go back and join your friends.

Why do I ask you to come forward publicly? We do everything else in public. But in addition to that Jesus said, "If you're not willing to acknowledge Me before men, I'll not acknowledge you before my Father." There's something about coming forward publicly out from the crowd and saying, "I receive Christ." It settles it in your heart.

I'm going to ask you to come. If you're with friends or relatives, they'll wait. You may be a member of the church; you may not be a member of any church. If you come from the top balcony up there, you have to go back and then down and around. An usher will show you. But all the other people can come straight down to the front and just come and stand here. Young man, young woman, father, mother. Whoever you are, whatever you are, God has spoken to you tonight. You get up and come right now and I'm going to ask that all of us be in an attitude of prayer as people come right now. Quickly, and just stand here reverently and say "Tonight I want Christ."[29]

In this sample invitation, typical of thousands that Graham has extended over the years, two characteristics stand out. First, the call to come forward is a call to receive Jesus Christ as Lord and Savior. By coming forward the sinner is openly acknowledging that he inwardly desires to repent, trust Christ, and live for Him. This does not mean that Billy Graham equates coming forward with salvation—although he has been accused of such a heresy.[30] In a published statement, he responded to the charge:

There's nothing about the mechanics of coming forward that saves anybody's soul. Coming forward is an open acknowledgment and a testimony of an inward experience that you have had with Christ. But this inward experience with Christ, this encounter, is the most important thing.[31]

Graham believes that those desiring to be saved should be willing to confess that desire publicly. Coming forward is an outward expression of an inward decision.

Second, Billy Graham's invitation includes an explanation to his audience why he calls them forward. A call alone for a public response will not suffice. People want and deserve to know why such an appeal is being made—what the logic and reasoning behind it are. Graham offers a variety of satisfying reasons. He explains that Jesus, while on earth, always called people publicly; that He commanded men to confess Him openly without shame. Often Billy will say, "There's something about coming forward publicly that settles it." He may point out that since man sinned in public, so he needs to be forgiven in public; or that Christ died publicly on the cross, and now He calls men to live publicly for Him.

After describing the reasons and necessity for making a public commitment to Christ, Graham makes his final appeal and quietly waits for the response. In what seems like only a few seconds to onlookers, but an eternity to Billy Graham, those desirous of salvation leave their seats and begin to make their way toward the front.

Between the time he closes his invitation and the time it takes for people to respond, Billy Graham experiences a great spiritual battle. In a private interview with this writer, he confided, "I cannot tell you the pressure I experience within. Suddenly I am made aware of the forces of evil and the forces of good, which are fighting for men's souls."[32] It is during this interval that Billy Graham becomes the target of a demonic onslaught. Often doubts flood his soul. "Will anyone come? Will anyone respond to the invitation?" he asks himself.[33] Just as suddenly the doubts are swept away as the Divine Comforter, the Holy Spirit, fills his heart with faith. Billy then enters into a state of total concentration and prayer.[34] He summarizes his intense feelings:

> I like to pray after the invitation is extended. It's at this
> point that I feel a real struggle with the enemy. The Bible

says, "But if our gospel be hid, it is hid to them that are lost: in whom the god of this world hath blinded the minds of them which believe not, lest the light of the glorious gospel of Christ, who is the image of God, should shine unto them" (2 Corinthians 4:3,4). Not only do I feel the need to pray, but I ask my associates and others to be much in prayer at this time as the battle rages for the souls of men.[35]

Guests who sit on the platform at a Billy Graham crusade meeting are asked to assemble one-half hour prior to the service, when they are given specific instructions to pray during invitation time for souls to be won to Christ.

Why Are Billy Graham's Invitations So Effective?

Theories for Graham's success in drawing people to Christ are many, ranging from the ridiculous to the logical. Some of his critics have suggested that his secret has been his good looks, his all-American appeal, his hypnotic eyes.[36] Such explanations are worthy of little or no comment, except to say that when Graham stands on second base to preach to a crowd of fifty thousand people, no one is close enough to notice his facial features or to look into his eyes. Other critics have speculated that his voice has a mesmeric quality about it that enables Graham to draw people to himself as would a spiritual pied piper. But how does such a hypothesis explain the hundreds of deaf people who receive Graham's message and invitation totally through sign language? Alistair Cooke, famous author and onetime reporter for the *Manchester Guardian,* has suggested that Billy uses "seduction" to lure his followers forward. This theory fails to account for the thousands who must sit in overflow auditoriums when the main arena is filled to capacity, yet who still respond to the invitation to receive Christ. Never seeing Graham, they receive his gospel message piped through a public address system. Seduction could hardly occur under such circumstances.

Nor can the critics account for the effectiveness of those Graham invitations, given in foreign crusades, which are filtered through one or more interpreters. Can charm, good looks, an all-American mystique, hypnotic eyes, or a seductive voice offer an adequate explanation? Obviously not.

A Divine Calling

Billy Graham believes that God has sovereignly called him and equipped him to evangelize the world. He feels he is on a divine mission, sent forth by the King of heaven and earth. The success of his mission is guaranteed. Discussing his role as a world evangelist, Graham comments:

> I believe, with all my heart as I look back on my life, that I was chosen to do this particular work . . . I believe that God in His sovereignty—I have no other answer for this—sheer sovereignty, chose me to do this work and prepared me in His own way.[37]

Philip Santora of the *New York Daily News* sees Graham as "a dedicated person who believes in what he is teaching, whose aim in life is to harvest as many souls as possible."[38] Santora's analysis is correct. As God's ambassador to the world, called to be an evangelist, Billy has one primary goal: to reap God's harvest. He has remarked, reminiscing about his early years, "I had one passion, and that was to win souls. I didn't have a passion to be a great preacher; I had a passion to win souls. I'd never been trained as a public speaker. I had to learn in the best way I knew."[39]

A Divine Message

The Cross of Christ is the central theme of all of Graham's evangelistic sermons. He realizes that an effective invitation cannot be extended unless it is preceded by the preaching of the gospel. Any message devoid of the *kērygma* will yield little or no lasting results.[40] Billy recounts how he learned this lesson the hard way:

> I was preaching in Dallas, Texas. We had the Cotton Bowl, a big stadium. On this particular evening it was about half-filled, and I preached my heart out. There was very little power in the service, and I knew it. I struggled and tried to get across a message, but very few people responded to the appeal. After the service, my good friend John Bolten rode with me back to the hotel. He said, "Billy, there was no power in the service tonight." I said, "No, John." He said, "Would you mind if I tell you why?" I said, "Please tell me." He said, "Billy, you didn't preach the Cross. . . . In evangelistic preaching there is no message outside the Cross." I determined that in every evangelistic sermon I preached from then on there would be the Cross.[41]

Billy has been careful to keep that promise. In the few instances when he has failed to preach on the Cross, he has noticed the effectiveness of his invitation blunted. In a letter to his wife, Ruth, he once wrote:

> The invitation was a little more difficult last night, and fewer people came. The moment I walked down from the platform the Holy Spirit said to me, "You did not preach Christ and the Cross as you should." I looked back over my sermon and I remembered that I had exalted Christ a little less, perhaps, and it was one of the few occasions that I did not touch on His death, burial, and resurrection as the heart of the message. The Lord taught me a lesson.[42]

Graham's faithfulness in preaching the good news is one of the key reasons for his successful invitations. He seldom strays off the topic. As Dr. Leslie Weatherhead once commented,

Billy "wisely realizes that men are changed by news, not views."[43]

A Divine Arsenal

One of Billy's greatest strengths is his constant "sense of inadequacy."[44] Over the years he has come to realize that he cannot humanly persuade anyone to come to Christ. He has learned to depend upon God's power alone—mediated through the Holy Spirit, prayer, and His Word—to draw men to Christ. Billy has said:

> I used to think that in evangelism I had to do it all, but now I approach evangelism with a totally different attitude. I approach it with complete relaxation. First of all, I don't believe any man can come to Christ unless the Holy Spirit has prepared his heart. . . . I don't believe any man can come to Christ unless God draws him. My job is to proclaim the message.[45]

Billy Graham is absolutely dependent upon the Spirit of God to prepare, convict, and persuade hearts, turning them to Christ. Graham does not plead or beg people to be reconciled to God; he trusts the Holy Spirit to do the drawing.

Graham's second spiritual weapon is prayer; not only his own prayers, but the prayers of people around the world. Through *Decision* magazine, Billy asks his four million friends and supporters to pray for each crusade. The Billy Graham Evangelistic Association also places full-page advertisements in other evangelical magazines months prior to a major evangelistic crusade, asking readers to pray that many would come to Christ. Quite possibly, each crusade city becomes the most prayed-over spot on earth.

During the crusade itself, hundreds of prayer groups meet daily to pray for souls. Only eternity will reveal the effects that millions of prayers have had on Billy Graham's effectiveness in calling people to Christ.

A few individuals have even devoted their lives to the task of praying for Billy Graham. One such saint of God was Pearl Goode, who in 1954 began praying for Graham's success. Pollock writes of her:

> She would travel by bus to the place of a crusade in America; friends sometimes raised money for her to fly. "She came to every crusade" is Ruth Graham's memory. "She never bothered Bill, but she would pray, all night some nights. In Copenhagen she had to sit in a tub of hot water to keep warm, but she prayed." When Pearl Goode died in 1972 Ruth gave an address at her funeral. Pointing to the casket she said, "Here lie the mortal remains of one of the secrets of Bill's success."[46]

Finally, Billy Graham believes that God's Word will not return void; hence, he uses it often. In a sermon entitled "The Cross," Billy quotes directly from the Bible twenty-three times, out of fifteen different books.[47] One sermon on the subject of sin includes thirty-two direct quotes from Scripture. Speaking of his frequent use of the Bible, Graham said, "It [the Bible] became a rapier and a sword in my hand that I have used to break open the hearts of men and to direct them to the Lord Jesus Christ."[48]

Graham knows that faith is produced through hearing the Word of God (Romans 10:17). Therefore, he speaks forth the Word in boldness, expecting the Holy Spirit to use it to regenerate hearts.

A Divine Enablement

When asked by the author if he felt he had a special gift of inviting people to Christ, Graham replied, "Yes. It is part of the gift of an evangelist."[49] Dr. G. Campbell Morgan would have agreed with Billy's response. He said:

> But is the proclamation all? By no means! The evangelist must constrain men to obey. There must be that wonderful wooing note that breaks men's hearts, and sweeps them to Christ. That is the final and most remarkable note of the real evangelist, by which he constrains men. Not merely the declaration of the evangel, not merely the announcement of the Lordship of Christ, and the declaration of the Cross, but the ability to take hold of men, and compel them to Christ.[50]

By this definition, Billy Graham is an evangelist *par excellence*. He has an amazing ability to win men to Christ. Graham confides, "I am convinced that God has called me to be a New Testament evangelist."[51]

> I have a responsibility and an obligation to give people the opportunity to decide "Yes" or "No." And when a man deliberately faces Christ and turns Him down, he can never be the same again . . . Jesus pushed the rich young ruler into a corner. He had to decide. He decided "No."[52]

Coupled with Billy Graham's calling as an evangelist is a divinely-bestowed ability to extend the gospel invitation. Walter Smyth, director of Graham's overseas crusade ministry, observes, "The one great gift that God has given Billy Graham is the gift of the invitation. There is no earthly reason for those people to come forward, but they do."[53] A friend remarked that even during his early years as a pastor, Billy "had the gift of getting people to respond in faith."[54] Graham has attempted to explain why his invitation has been effective:

> At the invitation I believe that God has given me the gift in asking people to come forward and make a com-

mitment to Christ at the end of my sermons. And in the several minutes that this appeal lasts . . . while I am standing there, not saying a word, it's when most of my strength leaves me. I have no explanation for that.[55]

Few would argue with Graham's own assessment: "I've always felt that what little sovereign gift I have is at that moment."[56]

What is the unique ability that Graham possesses? It is the gift of exhortation (see Chapter 3) in operation. Billy has been given a supernaturally-endowed ability to call sinners to Christ. He exhorts his listeners to "come quickly," "now," "tonight." His invitation is to the individual, not to the masses. Graham constantly uses the second person personal pronoun "you." He urges, *"You* come, from wherever *you* are. If *you* are with friends or relatives, they'll wait. *You* may be a member of a church, or attend no church at all. God is calling *you* to receive Christ." Billy Graham offers his appeal warmly, yet earnestly. People know he means business.

As Graham extends the public invitation, the Spirit of God empowers him in a special way. To his friend Roy Gustafson, he once remarked, "Roy, when I come to my invitation I sense God come on me, and I feel a power at that invitation that's peculiar."[57] Even the casual observer senses something supernatural transpiring as Billy extends the invitation. Crusade spectators witness firsthand the ministry and effects of a highly developed gift of exhortation being manifested before their eyes.

A key passage of Scripture which explains the operation of gifts is 1 Corinthians 12:4–6:

Now there are diversities of gifts, but the same Spirit. And there are differences of administrations, but the same Lord. And there are diversities of operations, but it is the same God which worketh all in all.

Note three significant truths. First, there is a variety of gifts (v. 4). Of course, the gift of exhortation is one of them (Romans 12:8). Second, these gifts can be administered in many different ways (v. 5). For example, one person can use his gift of exhortation in evangelism (Acts 2:40), while another uses his to minister to the saints (Acts 14:22). Finally, there are diversities of operations for each gift (v. 6). The Greek word for "operations" is *energēma,* from which the English word "energy" is derived. It means to be energized or empowered.

The various gifts are energized by God; He provides them with power, each gift energized at a level determined and regulated by Him who empowers it according to His will. A. T. Robertson concludes, therefore, that each gift produces a different result according to the power supplied it by God.[58] This offers a helpful insight into understanding why Billy Graham's exhortations produce such amazing results.

Various gifts are ministered in various ways with varying degrees of power. It is obvious that Graham's gift of exhortation is endued with a greater measure of power than most other evangelists. One observer of Billy's ministry said, "Graham's brother-in-law, Leighton Ford, gives a better-structured sermon, but the people come forward for Billy Graham. All others have to coax."[59] Graham's associate evangelists have noted that their invitations elicit a significantly smaller percentage of responses than do Billy's appeals. One associate summarized his colleagues' feelings when he said, "All of us would recognize the unusual gift that God has given to Billy."[60]

Ruth Graham once analyzed her husband's ability to win people to Christ by saying, "You weren't impressed with his earnestness, you weren't impressed with his gestures. You were impressed that there was Someone speaking to you besides Bill. There was another voice than his."[61] Ruth was referring to the voice of God. Her keen insight further confirms that Billy Graham has the gift of exhortation. The Apostle Paul described the operation of the gift when he wrote: "Now then we are ambassadors for Christ, as though *God did beseech* [*parakaleō*—"exhort"] *you by us;* we pray you in Christ's stead, be ye reconciled to God" (2 Corinthians 5:20 italics added). A prime characteristic of the gift of exhortation is that God uses the mouth of the evangelist to urge people to be saved.

Pollock records how the late Joe Blinco, one of Graham's associate evangelists, was conducting a crusade in Australia in 1959. One evening Graham attended the service. Afterward, he commented to Blinco, "Joe, when you gave the invitation, I wanted to stand up where I was and plead with the people and say 'Come!' "[62] Billy Graham's basic urge was not to preach the gospel, *but to extend the invitation,* to offer an exhortation. In his case, it is a gift which has been supercharged by God.

Graham has traveled far and wide to preach the gospel. He has addressed people of various national backgrounds and colors. He has delivered the good news of Christ in his native tongue and through as many as twenty interpreters at once. The universal message of God's love has been carried to Hindu, Buddhist, animist and atheist alike. Graham has presented the gospel in lands where evangelism was virtually unknown, and in countries where the public invitation was frowned upon. He has spoken to radicals, skeptics, theological liberals, militants, the intelligentsia, as well as the faithful. His messages have been preached in temperatures ranging from below freezing to 110°, and in the midst of torrential downpours. Under circumstances too numerous to mention, Graham has been faithful to deliver the *kērygma* and extend the invitation.

And people respond to Graham's simple call to receive Christ publicly. For some it means tramping through the rain; for others, it means laying aside lifelong religious beliefs. Many are forced to face the jeers and criticisms of their friends and families. A few pay the highest price of all—loss of life itself. Yet, they all flock forward when Billy Graham issues his appeal.

Regardless of the circumstances, Graham's invitation produces results. Even during illness, when his strength only allows him to preach ten or fifteen minutes, God's power takes over during the invitation.

Only one evangelist in modern church history has been able to turn such great numbers of people to Christ.* William Franklin Graham, Jr., is God's chief ambassador to the world.

---

* In Crusades held from 1947 through 1983, a total of 1,924,535 inquirers have publicly responded to Mr. Graham's invitation to receive Christ. Source: The Billy Graham Evangelistic Association, Minneapolis, Minnesota.

6

Answering the Critics

One of this century's most vocal opponents of the public invitation was the late Dr. D. Martyn Lloyd-Jones, successor to G. Campbell Morgan as senior pastor at Westminster Chapel, London, England.[1] His book *Preaching and Preachers* lists nine reasons for his opposition to the practice. As Lloyd-Jones was a leading spokesman for Reformed thought, his arguments against the public invitation can be considered representative of the movement as a whole.

Were Dr. Lloyd-Jones' objections to the public invitation valid criticisms? Let's look at each in turn.

First, the public invitation is wrong, Dr. Lloyd-Jones holds, because it puts direct pressure on the human will.[2] He explains that the inner man is comprised of three entities: intellect, emotions, and will. The will, he insists, must never be approached directly, but only indirectly by first going through the intellect and the emotions:

> Truth is addressed primarily to the mind. As the mind grasps it, and understands it, the affections are kindled and moved, and so in turn the will is persuaded and obedience is the outcome. In other words the obedience is not the result of direct pressure on the will, it is the result of an enlightened mind and a softened heart. To me this is a crucial point.[3]

While Dr. Lloyd-Jones is correct in stressing the importance of approaching the will through the mind and emotions, his observation does not eliminate the necessity for extending a public invitation. Instead, he underscores the truism that no invitation should be issued which has not been preceded by a clear gospel presentation. It seems that, at this point, Lloyd-Jones is opposed to improper use of the invitation—i.e., those invitations which attempt to coerce or manipulate people rather than move them on the basis of the gospel message alone.

Second, Dr. Lloyd-Jones postulates that many people who come forward are responding because of the personality of the evangelist, general fear, or psychological influences, and not for spiritual reasons.[4] This argument is difficult to prove or disprove, since it is next to impossible to judge accurately inquirers' motives for coming forward. Undoubtedly, many evangelists have used the tactic of undue fear, or have practiced mass psychology on their audiences. That is tragic; but it does not negate the legitimate use of invitations. Lloyd-Jones' second objection, like his first, is more of a disagreement with invitational abuses, than with the principle of the invitation itself.

Third, Dr. Lloyd-Jones objects to the public invitation on the basis that it is tacked on to a sermon, thus dividing the proclamation into two distinct parts.[5] He states that the preaching of the Word and the call for decisions cannot be separated, a point no professor of homiletics would dispute. Every evangelistic message should include both the *kērygma* and a challenge to repent and believe.

What Lloyd-Jones so vehemently opposes is not a call to repent and believe (which he considers proper and valid) but the concept of asking people to come forward as an outward indication of an inward change. This is what he feels is improperly tacked on. The only possible answer to this criticism is that Dr. Lloyd-Jones' argument is with the Bible rather than with some modern-day method of evangelism. On the day of Pentecost, Peter, filled with the Holy Spirit, not only preached the gospel, but called upon his listeners to repent and publicly present themselves for believer's baptism. The Apostle's call to repent included a call for public action. There is a definite biblical basis for extending a public invitation.

The fourth argument advanced against the public invitation is that the practice carries with it the implication that sinners have an inherent power to come to Christ, which they do not.[6] Lloyd-Jones forcefully argues that since lost man is spiritually dead in trespasses and sins, he is unable to respond to the invitation (1 Corinthians 2:14; Ephesians 2:1). A dead man does not possess the ability to raise himself to life! Dr. Lloyd-Jones believes that the issuing of the public invitation is a call to "self-conversion."

Dr. Lloyd-Jones' premise—that the natural man does not have the capacity to save himself—is certainly valid. Man is totally and unequivocally lost apart from divine intervention. When Jesus' disciples came to realize this important truth, they asked, "Who then can be saved?" (Matthew 19:25). To which Jesus responded, "With men this is impossible; but *with God* all things are possible" (Matthew 19:26).

Through the power of the Word and the ministry of the Holy Spirit, man's mind is enlightened to receive the gospel and his will freed to respond. That which is impossible to man becomes possible through the power of God. As evangelist Leighton Ford brings out so clearly:

> If anyone feels that he cannot give an invitation for a sinner to come to Christ, because of man's inability, let him remember that Jesus invited a man whose hand was paralyzed to do what he could not do! "... Stretch out your hand ..." Jesus commanded (Matthew 12:13), and the man obeyed the command and did what he could not do! Let him remember also that Jesus told a dead man to

do something he could not do—to live! ". . . Lazarus, come forth," He commanded (John 11:43), and Lazarus obeyed the voice of Jesus and did what he could not do.[7]

At the invitation time God speaks through the evangelist, calling the spiritually dead to come to life (2 Corinthians 5:20). It is God, not man, who resurrects the soul and enables man to live.

As a fifth criticism, Lloyd-Jones declares that most evangelists who issue invitations are attempting to manipulate the Holy Spirit.[8] Exactly what Dr. Lloyd-Jones means is unclear, since he does not fully expand upon his argument. Possibly he means that many evangelists try to overcome their listeners' resistance and, rather than allow the Spirit to do His work in His own time, attempt to get *additional* people to respond to the invitation. In his zeal, the evangelist may try to manipulate the Spirit to draw those He had not intended to draw. If this is what Lloyd-Jones means by "manipulating" the Holy Spirit, then he is touching on the matter of election.

The doctrine of election is a belief that only those chosen by God will be saved. It is a doctrine that has no bearing whatsoever on the issuing of a public invitation. The evangelist is commissioned to preach the gospel to all peoples and to issue the call to all peoples (Mark 16:15; John 3:16). He is to exhort, "Whosoever will, let him take the water of life freely" (Revelation 22:17). He is to explain that those who do not heed the call will be held personally responsible, and forced to suffer the consequences of their willful rebellion (John 3:18,36).

The evangelist does not try to manipulate his listeners, or coerce the Holy Spirit to act against His will. As an ambassador of the King of the universe, he simply delivers the King's proclamation and waits for the reply. The doctrines of election and free will are not the issues.

Sixth, Dr. Lloyd-Jones argues that people come forward not because they are under conviction of sin, but because they want to obtain certain positive benefits, i.e., acceptance by family, to escape judgment.[9] Once again, it is virtually impossible to assess a person's motive for responding to a public invitation. The evangelist can eliminate people coming for the wrong reasons if he is careful to give precise instructions during his invitation. He needs to explain fully that through the invitation God is calling sinners to repent and trust Christ publicly for salvation. Another preventive step is to make sure that those who come forward are thoroughly dealt with by a counselor or personal worker to ascertain why the inquirer responded. The gospel can then again be explained and the seeker challenged to repent and believe on Christ.

Lloyd-Jones' seventh objection is that the public invitation encourages people to think they are saved by going forward.[10] Though no New Testament evangelist believes or teaches that a walk to the front of the auditorium saves anyone, in the minds of many of the unregenerated, this is not the case. Therefore, it is imperative that the evangelist inform his audience, prior to or during the invitation, that coming forward saves no one. He needs to explain further that a public response to the gospel is only an outward expression of an inward desire on the part of the hearer to repent and believe.

The eighth criticism offered by Martyn Lloyd-Jones is that the public invitation supplants the work of the Holy Spirit.[11] (Earlier, Lloyd-Jones said the evangelist tries to *manipulate* the Spirit; now he argues that the evangelist, through the public invitation, attempts to *replace* the Holy Spirit.) Lloyd-Jones believes the job of the evangelist is to preach the gospel, while the ministry of the Spirit is to convict of sin, call, and draw sinners to Christ. By issuing a public invitation the evangelist, Lloyd-Jones contends, is making an effort to do the Spirit's job.

The ministries of the evangelist and the Spirit cannot be so neatly categorized and separated. Rather than working exclusive of each other, they are united. The evangelist is a fellow-worker with the Holy Spirit. Together they preach, convince, persuade, and call men to Christ. The Apostle Paul said to Timothy, "The Lord *stood with me* that all the Gentiles might hear" (2 Timothy 4:17). To the Colossians he wrote:

> We preach, warning every man, and teaching every man in all wisdom; that we may present every man perfect in Christ Jesus: whereunto I also labour, striving according to *His working which worketh in me* mightily.
>
> (Colossians 1:28,29)

Paul was indwelt by the presence of God, who spoke through him to win souls. Immediately following the Great Commission, the gospel writer Mark records: "And they went forth, and preached every where, *the Lord working with them*" (Mark 16:20). John the revelator closes his final book with the exhortation, "The Spirit *and* the bride say, Come" (Revelation 22:17). Whether in preaching the gospel or issuing the invitation, the evangelist sees his efforts as being one with the Spirit indwelling him. The evangelist is sensitive to the Spirit's leading and is totally dependent upon Him for the results. As C. E. Autrey logically deducts, "The evangelist is not pushing the Holy Spirit aside when he pleads in the invitation any more than when he prepares and delivers the body of the sermon."[12]

Dr. D. Martyn Lloyd-Jones' final objection to the public invitation is that no sinner ever "decides" for Christ.[13] Here Lloyd-Jones is hung up on terminology. He emphasizes that nowhere in the Bible can be found an admonition to decide for Christ or to accept Christ. Rather than man choosing God, God chooses man. While this century's foremost critic of the public invitation is technically correct, he fails to mention that God also holds each person who hears the gospel accountable for his response. The sinner has a choice to either accept or reject the claims of Christ.

Although not explicitly stated, it may be that Lloyd-Jones is arguing in favor of the doctrine of irresistible grace. When God calls, man *must* respond positively. He has no choice in the matter. In this sense, he does not decide for Christ. The decision has already been made for him.

Most evangelists have difficulty, on biblical grounds, in accepting this doctrine without serious reservations. To present the argument for the sovereignty of God without equally presenting the argument for man's responsibility is to paint only half the picture. It is true that God is sovereign, but it is equally true that He holds each man personally responsible for his eternal destiny. J. I. Packer offers a balanced explanation:

> As King, He orders and controls all things, human actions among them, in accordance with His own eternal purpose. Scripture also teaches that, as Judge, He holds every man responsible for the choices he makes and the courses of action he pursues. Thus, the hearers of the gospel are responsible for their reaction; if they reject the good news, they are guilty of unbelief. . . . God made us responsible moral agents, and He will not treat us as anything less.[14]

The evangelist presents the message that "God ... now commandeth all men every where to repent" (Acts 17:30). He then issues the appeal for sinners to obey God's command and be saved. His appeal is urgent as he calls upon his listeners to respond immediately: "Today if ye will hear his voice, harden not your hearts" (Hebrews 3:7,8). The evangelist lays the responsibility upon his hearers, not God, for their salvation: *they* must choose.

Whether or not the evangelist subscribes to the doctrine of irresistible grace, he is to preach the gospel and call upon his listeners to repent and believe. It is not his job to figure out who the saved will be, or to issue a limited appeal. His task is to present the gospel to *every* creature, coupling it with the invitation that "whosoever will" may come. Speaking as an evangelist, Stephen Olford observes:

> There is nothing more thrilling in all the world than to issue the call of the gospel and to see men and women believe. [The] . . . redemptive invitation of God demands a verdict. Man can never confront the gospel of the Lord Jesus Christ and remain indifferent, apathetic or aloof. He has to decide. With the revelation and invitation of the gospel man has to give an answer. If he believes he is saved; if he rejects he is lost.[15]

Dr. D. Martyn Lloyd-Jones, although a staunch critic of the public invitation, did issue an appeal at the end of his evangelistic messages for listeners to repent and believe. While not calling them forward, he did exhort them to meet with him in private after the church service or in his office the next morning. Also, Dr. Lloyd-Jones was a strong advocate of personal evangelism and soul winning. As Billy Graham once commented:

> We have noticed that some who are against public evangelistic invitations go to almost any length using the appeal in personal evangelism. If it is right to ask a single sinner to repent and receive the Lord Jesus Christ, why is it not right to ask a whole audience to do the same?[16]

7

Extending a Public Invitation—The Reasons Why

Proponents of the public invitation greatly outnumber its critics. Why do so many pastors and evangelists feel the need to extend a call to their listeners to appropriate the gospel publicly to their lives?

Scriptural Reasons*

Men, women and children (who have reached the age of accountability) need Christ, or they will perish eternally. God has chosen in His infinite wisdom to use human vessels to reach these lost ones with the message of His redeeming love. Not only does God commission preachers to carry the gospel to every creature, He also commissions them to issue a call to rebellious men to respond positively to the gospel. The proclamation and the invitation cannot be separated. The Apostle Paul showed the connection between the two when he wrote: "For . . . it pleased God by the foolishness of preaching to save them that believe. . . . But unto them which are called, both Jews and Greeks, Christ the power of God, and the wisdom of God" (1 Corinthians 1:21,24). Commenting on this important passage, Dr. Stephen F. Olford writes:

* See Chapter 4 for additional scriptural support of the public invitation.

139

> There are two words that sum up the divine process in the invitation of the gospel. The one is the word "called," and the other is the word "believe." The one describes the offer of God: He calls; it is His effectual call. The other denotes the response of man: he believes, he commits himself.[1]

Through the proclamation of the gospel, God speaks to hearts (John 16:8; Acts 24:25); through the invitation, He beseeches men to be reconciled to Himself (2 Corinthians 5:20). The gospel presentation demands a verdict. To deliver the *kērygma* only, without issuing an invitation, is to be disobedient to the Great Commission (Matthew 28:19). As Dr. C. Sumner Wemp has said, "We preach not to inform but to transform our listeners."[2]

A second scriptural reason for giving a public invitation is to afford those who have heard the gospel in the past an opportunity to receive Christ. Lost people are at various stages in their relationship to Christ. Some have never heard the gospel; they are in total darkness. Others are on the verge of making a commitment. They have sat in churches for many years hearing the gospel expounded, or may have been exposed to the evangel through literature, radio, television, or films. They are ready to receive Christ. The public invitation offers them an immediate opportunity to do so. Scripture is clear that evangelism includes the *planting* or sowing of the seed of God's Word (1 Corinthians 3:6), at which time the sinner hears the gospel for the first time. It also includes *watering* (1 Corinthians 3:6), when the sinner is further exposed to gospel truth and it is explained to his understanding. He also becomes the subject of many prayers that the Word will take root, grow, and produce faith. Unfortunately, many evangelistic efforts stop here. The New Testament pattern includes another step: *harvesting,* when the invitation is extended for the sinner to repent and trust Christ (John 4:35,36). Through the invitation, God gives the increase (1 Corinthians 3:7) and adds new members to His Church (Acts 2:47).

By giving an invitation, the pastor or evangelist can reap a harvest of souls that was planted weeks, months, and even years earlier. Dr. James A. Stewart explains that when evangelist D. L. Moody came to Scotland in the late 1890s, his efforts were greatly blessed by God because he was preaching to people who had heard the gospel all their lives. They knew they needed to repent and believe, but they did not know how to go about it. When Moody extended his public invitation, they flocked forward by the thousands to receive help for their seeking souls.

Finally, through precept and example the Scriptures enjoin God's servants to issue a public invitation. The Bible opens with God seeking the fellowship of fallen man through a call (Genesis 3:9). It closes with God and the church issuing a final appeal for sinners to come to Christ (Revelation 22:17). The task that God began alone, He expects the church to continue. Dr. I. D. E. Thomas, a pastor with strong Puritan and Reformed leanings, says he issues a public invitation because "we are bidden to persuade, command, even compel them to come in."[3]

Historical Reasons

There are historical precedents for extending a public invitation. The Old Testament records the history of God's dealings with His people, Israel. Through the nation's numerous leaders, God called His people to publicly gather in a display of faithfulness to Him. Roland Leavell offers the interesting hypothesis that the Old Testament prophets were the equivalent of today's evangelists. They pressed their listeners to repent and take an immediate public stand for God. John the Baptist, God's last prophet under the Old Testament dispensation, is a good example of this theory's contention. He pointed men to the Messiah, called upon them to repent and to prove their faithfulness by submitting to baptism. The gospel writer Matthew records: "Then went out to him Jerusalem, and all Judea, and all the region around about Jordan, and were baptized of him in Jordan, confessing their sins" (Matthew 3:5,6).

The public invitation did not stop with the Old Testament prophets. Jesus continued the practice, baptizing and calling men unto Himself (John 4:1,2; Matthew 11:28,29). He was followed by the early apostles, who likewise called men to publicly repent and believe (Acts 2:38). They were succeeded by the early evangelists, who took the gospel into the highways and invited sinners to publicly come to Christ (Acts 8:1,12, 35–38). The first pastors carried on the apostolic tradition, exhorting sinners to stand by their side as a public indication of their desire to follow Christ (2 Timothy 4:5). When the apostolic age came to a close, God called others to evangelize the world. Despite criticism, persecution, and oftentimes death, these brave men called upon sinners to make an open confession of their faith. History's greatest soul-winning evangelists have used some type of public invitation. The public invitation has historically stood the test of time as a method used and blessed of God to bring people to His Son, Jesus Christ.

Practical Reasons

The public invitation is a practical way to accomplish the main task of evangelism: namely, winning people to Christ at the earliest possible moment. Every church has unbelievers attending its services. Some practical means is needed to reach these people with the gospel and deal with them personally about the eternal destiny of their souls. The public invitation provides such means. Dr. Charles Stanley, senior pastor of the First Baptist Church in Atlanta, Georgia, estimates that Christians comprise ninety-eight percent of his congregation on any given Sunday morning; yet he still issues an invitation. Amazingly, he has hundreds of converts each year through this method.[4]

A pastor should never assume that he is addressing believers only. God alone knows the human heart. Dr. G. Campbell Morgan warned:

> There is a danger that we take too much for granted about the people to whom we preach, and if we are not careful we shall drift into the opinion that because these people are attending services, therefore there is no need for the direct appeal of the evangel to be made to them. We must ever remember that it is necessary that every individual person should come into personal relationship with Jesus Christ.[5]

The public invitation allows those wanting to be saved an opportunity to seek help from a trained personal worker. It shows them that the church and pastor are concerned about their spiritual welfare, and lessens the likelihood that anyone in need will leave the sanctuary without receiving help and counsel.

A second practical reason for issuing the invitation is that some people come under such a strong conviction of sin during a gospel message that they miss half of what is said. All they know is that they want to be saved, but they are at a loss as to how to go about it. The public invitation gives them an opportunity to be helped.

Dr. Lewis Drummond, professor of evangelism at Southern Baptist Theological Seminary, writes, "I conceive the basic purpose of the invitation is to get the convicted forward to be dealt with on a personal basis for salvation. . . . This is the opportunity, in the old historical sense, for seekers and inquirers to come forward for counsel."[6] Here Drummond alludes to the public invitation used by Finney and others in the early nineteenth century, primarily as a means to deal effectively with people who were being convicted of sin by the Holy Spirit. Those who were "anxious" over their soul's salvation were invited to the "anxious bench." The public invitation today serves the same practical purpose.

Finally, a call for people to come forward is a useful means of offering help to people who have heard the complete gospel message, but remain confused about its meaning. By responding to the invitation, the confused person can receive a further explanation of the gospel and have his questions answered by a counselor. Dwight L. Moody viewed his invitation as a means to this end. He once commented:

> Some people say, "All you . . . [need] to do is to make preaching so plain that plain people will understand it." Well, Christ was a plain preacher, and yet he asked, "Have ye understood all these things?" (Matthew 13:51). He encouraged them to inquire. . . . We must have personal work—hand-to-hand work—if we are going to have results.[7]

The public invitation is practical. It has proven to be an effective method of bringing people to Christ.

Logical Reasons

The gospel demands a response. It calls upon man to make a choice. Will he accept or reject Jesus Christ? After hearing the claims and promises of Christ, a person cannot remain neutral for long. Failure to give the invitation permits the sinner to evade and postpone the action which God expects him to take immediately.

To fail to extend an invitation following a gospel sermon is not only blatant disobedience to God, but it also defies logic. Would a lawyer, defending his client, present all the pertinent evidence and then fail to plead with the jury to return a favorable verdict? The whole purpose of a lawyer's presentation is to win the case. Likewise, the evangelistic sermon is structured for the sole purpose of winning people to Christ. It is only logical, therefore, to ask them to make a decision on the spot. The late Dr. R. G. Lee, one of the South's great orators, once wrote to a friend:

> A clothier, seeking to fit suits of clothes on men, does not just talk of the quality of the suits, but he seeks to get people to buy. Flour salesmen do not just talk about the goodness of flour and the worth of the bread made therefrom, but they seek to sell flour. Insurance agents do not use many words as to the security and assets of the company, but they seek to get people to take out insurance policies.
>
> Preachers need to be salesmen of the gospel. That is the greatest commodity known on earth and in heaven.[8]

Robert Sumner summarizes the weight of reason: "All of logic is against telling someone to do something without pressing him to act immediately."[9] It might be added that it is just as illogical not to provide him with an *opportunity* to act.

Psychological Reasons

Man needs an outlet for response. When the heart is stirred and the mind convinced, an avenue of expression must be provided. The invisible realities of the soul seek to express themselves through visible manifestations. George E. Sweazey, whose book on evangelism has been used for nearly three decades, has written on the need for tangible demonstration:

> Christ and the Bible and all Christian history have set certain outward signs to mark spiritual realities. Though there is a constant danger that the sign may become a

substitute for the reality, the risk must be taken because human minds have to have something tangible by which the intangible can be revealed. Love needs weddings and education needs diplomas and patriotism needs a flag—and Christianity needs sacraments and open professions of faith and religious practices.

Evangelism's good work is likely to be lost if it takes the outward signs too casually.[10]

W. E. Grindstaff has similarly commented: "Nothing is more cruel and damaging than to disturb people religiously, make them ready for decision, and then fail to give an invitation to register the decision."[11] To do so is to leave souls burdened and psyches frustrated. It is possibly for this reason that many psychiatrists and psychologists have written to Billy Graham commending him for issuing a public invitation.[12] It is psychologically sound. Whatever act is used to symbolize a decision for Christ—a spoken statement, the signing of a card, the raising of a hand, the walk down a church aisle—it allows the will to express itself.

A second psychological reason for giving a public invitation is that people are mentally conditioned to expect it. Billy Graham perceptively observes:

We live in a day of skillful and high-pressure advertising. People are accustomed to all kinds of appeals from television, radio, newspapers, magazines, and billboards. They are bringing a flood of solicitations to see and buy. Salesmen ask us to sign on the dotted line when their sales appeal ends. Our generation is perhaps more invitation-minded in this respect than any other has ever been. It seems to me that we as a Church today could use this invitation-consciousness at every favorable evangelistic opportunity.[13]

To present the gospel, extol the benefits of accepting Christ, and then not issue an appeal for people to respond is bound to leave them confused and disappointed. They have been psychologically conditioned to expect an invitation; indeed, they want one to be given.

Finally, a public invitation is a psychological aid to the memory, for both those who respond and those who do not. A public commitment to Christ can never be forgotten, while a mental affirmation can. This may be what Billy Graham means when he says, "There is something about coming forward that settles it." The believer who trusts Christ publicly carries with him a vivid picture of the time and circumstances of his conversion. Whenever he is tempted by the enemy to turn his back on God, or begins to doubt his salvation, he has a mental reminder of his surrender to the Lord.

For the unconverted, the public invitation presses the point of the gospel home in a concrete manner. It visibly reminds them that God expects their commitment. After the theological content of the evangelist's message has faded from memory, the picture of people going forward is still with them. They will continue to think "about the invitation, about their attitude toward it, about the stand they took, or did not take, long after they have forgotten most of what . . . [is] said in . . . [the] appeal."[14] The public invitation prepares the hearts of those who did not receive Christ to do so at a subsequent time.

Consequential Reasons

The public invitation produces positive results in the lives of onlookers. People are more readily moved by what they see than by a nebulous hope that some sinner may privately come to Christ in the future.

Effects Upon Christian Observers

The public invitation affects Christian observers in various ways. For some it brings to memory their own walk forward. It allows them to relive their commitment, and often motivates them to rededicate their lives privately to the Lord. Their hearts are kept warm toward evangelism and drawn closer to God.

Another positive effect is that the public invitation assures the Christian that the many lost friends he invites to church will be given an opportunity to be saved. It is an impetus to consistency and faithfulness in personal evangelism. And when the invitation is responded to, the Christian observer is encouraged to see that his prayers have not gone unanswered, and that his financial gifts to the church or crusade were not given in vain. In front of his eyes are the fruits of his labor.

People exposed to public invitations are often stirred to become soul winners. A chain reaction starts. A prime example is Tom Phillips, president of the Raytheon Corporation, saved during Billy Graham's New York Crusade in Madison Square Garden in June 1969. Several years later, he witnessed to Charles Colson of Watergate fame. Through Phillips' testimony and continued influence, Colson was won to Christ. He in turn has led thousands to the Lord.

Billy Sunday's public invitations had far-reaching results. Dr. John R. Rice remembers, "All over America, Billy Sunday campaigns resulted in 'Billy Sunday Clubs,' groups of businessmen converted in his campaigns who set out to win souls in jails, in street meetings, in the missions, and in personal interviews."[15]

Rice says that a Billy Sunday Club started in Binghamton, New York in 1926 was still going strong a decade later. Thirty-five of its members served as ushers in one of Dr. Rice's own crusades in the same city ten years later.[16]

"There is nothing that will encourage Christians to go out and work harder to reach others," writes Sumner, "than seeing what can happen. It gives them renewed desires and interest in working harder to reach the lost."[17]

Dr. William McCarrell, former pastor of the Cicero Bible Church near Chicago, stated that prior to 1922 he did not usually give invitations. After that year, he started issuing them on a regular basis. A spirit of revival and evangelistic fervor broke out among the congregation. McCarrell attributed the changes to the effects the public invitation had on his people.[18]

A fourth positive effect of the public invitation is that it moves Christians to renew their commitment to the Lord. The mayor of Indianapolis rededicated his life to Christ during the 1980 Billy Graham Indianapolis Crusade. The mayor, a platform guest, was emotionally moved as he saw the throngs of inquirers coming forward to be saved. The experience caused him to evaluate his own relationship with the Lord.[19]

And during the 1981 Greater Baltimore Billy Graham Crusade, the lieutenant governor of Maryland left his seat on the platform to take a place among other seekers on the field. He had made a decision for Christ at a youth rally when he was twelve. Touched by the sight of the public invitation, he moved forward to offer his life afresh to the Lord.

A final effect the public invitation has on many Christian observers is that it builds them up spiritually. As they see the miraculous happening before their very eyes, they are moved to join in the heavenly choruses of praise and rejoicing that echo throughout the universes (Luke 15:10). God calls out to Christians at harvest time: "Rejoice with me; for I have found my sheep which was lost" (Luke 15:6).

The moving effects the invitation has on Christians take many forms. Dr. Paige Patterson, of Dallas, Texas, relates the following true story:

> [When] our Russian Baptist brethren visited with us, . . . they sat on the platform and wept during the whole situation [the invitation], realizing that this is something that they could not do in the Soviet Union, but were deeply moved by the way people were responding to the Lord.[20]

Likewise, Dr. Helmut Thielicke, the well-known German theologian and preacher, attended one of Billy Graham's 1963 European Crusades. In a private letter to Mr. Graham, he expressed the feelings he had had as he sat on the platform and saw the thousands responding to the public invitation:

> Now I saw them all coming towards us, I saw there their assembled, moved and honestly decided faces, I saw their searching and their meditativeness. I confess that this moved me to the very limits. Above all there were two young men—a white and a negro—who stood at the front and about whom one felt that they were standing at that moment on Mount Horeb and looking from afar into a land they had longed for. I shall never forget those faces. It became lightning clear that men *want* to make a decision. . . . I shall have to draw from all this certain consequences in my own preaching, even though the outward form will of course look somewhat different.[21]

Effects Upon Pastors and Evangelists

One of the great rewards of those pastors and evangelists who extend a public invitation is they witness the lost being saved. The sight of people coming forward is an encouragement to preachers to continue faithfully toiling in the Word. It is also a very heartwarming and emotional experience.

The public invitation additionally allows the pastor or evangelist to measure the effectiveness of his presentation. If no one responds to his gospel sermons, some drastic changes obviously need to be made. Reactions to the appeal help the preacher to evaluate his ministry.

Finally, the public invitation gives the preacher immediate access to new converts. He is able to identify them, establish a friendship with them when possible, and offer needed spiritual assistance and counsel. It is far better to give people an opportunity to respond to a public invitation than to fail to give one and never know what their response might have been.

8

How to Prepare and Deliver a Public Invitation

Andrew W. Blackwood, master pulpiteer of a generation ago, believed that the most important portion of a sermon, apart from its text, is its conclusion.[1]

The ideal conclusion serves three primary purposes. First, it effectively brings the sermon to a close. Second, it applies the truth of the message to the lives of the listeners. It answers the question, "What does this sermon mean to me?" Third, the conclusion calls upon hearers to take an immediate action in response to the truth presented.

Ozora S. Davis defines the conclusion as "that part of the discourse in which the discussion is drawn to a close and the truth is fitted to life."[2] In evangelistic preaching, the public invitation serves as the conclusion for the sermon. As L. R. Scarborough correctly notes, "The invitation is the logical climax of the evangelistic sermon. Without it the message is incomplete and its effects unknown."[3]

If the conclusion is the most important structural part of the sermon, the invitation is the most important part of the evangelistic sermon. Every evangelistic message succeeds or fails according to the effectiveness of the invitation. The main goal of the gospel is to bring men and women into a saving relationship with Jesus Christ. If the invitation continually fails to produce this desired result, the sermon is considered to be less than successful. Dr. Charles W. Koller remarks:

> The supreme test of all preaching is: What happens to the man in the pew? To John the Baptist there was accorded the highest tribute that could ever come to a minister of the gospel: When they had heard John, "They followed Jesus" (John 1:37)[4].

Evangelistic preaching has no more important function than the issuing of an effective invitation. Yet, it is here that most ministers dismally fail. The reasons are many. Some pastors are afraid of being labeled a fanatic. Others are afraid of failure. Many have legitimate doubts as to the necessity of issuing a public invitation. Most fail, however, because they do not know how to give a good invitation. No college or seminary courses are offered on the subject. Few conferences on evangelism touch on this topic. The bookshelves are nearly bare when it comes to the all-important discussion of the public invitation.

Dr. Howard O. Jones, associate evangelist with the Billy Graham Evangelistic Association, believes that so little material is available on the invitation because so few preachers feel competent to write in this area.[5] This chapter will attempt to provide the interested and concerned evangelistic preacher with guidelines to help him construct and deliver an effective invitation.

How You Can Prepare an Effective Invitation

Every preacher of the gospel can extend an effective invitation, but it takes hard work. Not every minister has the gift of exhortation which would enable him to issue an appeal extemporaneously. This means, if you wish to succeed in winning souls to Christ through preaching, you must be willing to prepare and plan the invitation with the same care you do the main body of your sermon. Failing to prepare is preparing to fail. Through His inspiration and your perspiration the Holy Spirit can and will guide you to develop an invitation which can be used by Him to draw people to God's Son.

Prayer

Set a time aside for the purpose of preparing your invitation. Turn to God for help and guidance. You need to pray specifically for certain things. First, pray for yourself, that God will break your heart concerning the lost condition of many within your congregation or services. Someone once said that preaching should be spelled "pre-aching." The preacher without an ache in his heart for the lost will be unable to move them. Harry Saulnier, director of the world-famous Pacific Garden Mission, attributes a lack of concern about the souls of men to a lack or neglect of regular prayer.[6] Prayer is the key. The pastor or evangelist who wishes to be successful in drawing the net must first pray until God gives him a passion and burden for souls. Pray until you can say with the Apostle Paul:

> I say the truth in Christ, I lie not, my conscience also bearing me witness in the Holy Ghost, that I have great heaviness and continual sorrow in my heart. For I could wish that myself were accursed from Christ for my brethren, my kinsmen according to the flesh. (Romans 9:1–3)

As you commune with Christ through prayer, the concern the Lord has for the souls of men will become your concern. After reaching this point, much of the battle will be won. As Spurgeon said, "A burning heart will soon find for itself a flaming tongue."[7]

Pray for your flock; specifically, those who are without Christ. Before the preacher can effectively speak to men about God, he must first speak to God about men. As Scarborough points out:

> Pentecost's soul-saving conquests came after the continuous prayers of the Jerusalem church. All of Christ's earthly movements were marked by prayer. The successful ministries of all evangelists have been immersed in soulful supplication.[8]

Use a list of your members' names to identify those in need of salvation. Prayer should not end with your membership alone. You should also pray that God will send into your meetings others who need Christ.

Finally, you will want to pray for the Spirit's help in preparing and delivering an effective invitation. Much labor lies ahead; much divine assistance will be needed.

The Transition

The invitation begins where the proclamation ends. A great difficulty for many preachers is moving from the main body of the message into the invitation without an abrupt break. It is important that this transition be smooth. An apparent disjuncture in the sermon will distract the audience, drawing their attention to the sermon's structure and away from the message. If this happens, you will be forced to win back their attention. The way to avoid this is to use a connective or transitional statement.

One effective method of connecting the message to the invitation is by asking an appropriate question. This is the technique used by Billy Graham. The use of a connective question is especially adaptable to evangelistic sermons which have as their central theme the death, burial, and resurrection of

Christ. You may conclude your message with the challenge, "You have heard the truth. What are you going to do about it? You have to make a choice. You cannot remain neutral." This type of challenge allows you to move smoothly into the invitation, where you can invite people to make the correct choice. You may wish to ask a scriptural question such as, "What think ye of Christ?" (Matthew 22:42), "How long halt ye between two opinions?" (1 Kings 18:21), or, "What must I do to be saved?" (Acts 16:30). This method allows you to answer the question for your listeners as God would have them answer it.

Another type of transition is the promise. You can close the message portion of your sermon with the statement, "Now we come to the end of the sermon, but for you it can be a new beginning." Such a statement allows you to explain how in Christ they can become new creatures (2 Corinthians 5:17), be born again (John 3:3), put on the new man (Colossians 3:10), or be given a new heart (Ezekiel 36:26).

The various methods of making a smooth transition into the invitation are limited only by your imagination.

Theological Instructions

Once the transition has been successfully completed, it is imperative that you instruct your listeners how to be saved. Peter did not allow his audience's question, "What shall we do?" (Acts 2:37) to go unanswered. Neither should the preacher of the gospel. You must clearly and concisely explain to your listeners what God expects of them. You must call them to repent, believe, and follow Christ openly and unashamedly. These three points should be included in every gospel invitation. Under each category you need to define and illustrate your terms, and provide scriptural support. For example, the exhortation to repent can be illustrated by describing a soldier halting and making an "about face." You then explain that this is what God calls them to do. They must make an about face, turning away from their sin and false gods to the one true God. The scriptural basis is, "God ... now commandeth all men every where to repent" (Acts 17:30).

While the theological content of every gospel invitation will be the same—repent, believe, confess—the definitions can be freshly elaborated, the illustrations changed, and new Scriptures used from week to week.

The purpose of defining each word, providing a proper illustration, and offering biblical evidence, is for the sake of clarity. If people do not know what repent means, they will be confused and intellectually unable to take the necessary step toward salvation. Spurgeon once said, "We must preach in what Whitefield used to call 'market language' if we would have all classes of the community listening to our message."[9] Billy Sunday uttered these words of common sense: "Put the cookies on the lower shelf so everybody can reach them."[10] You cannot be too clear or simplistic when instructing your parishioners. It was said of Jesus, "The common people heard him gladly" (Mark 12:37). When asked by this writer what one piece of advice he would give pastors and evangelists to strengthen their invitations, Billy Graham replied, "Tell the people clearly what to do."[11]

The Proper Use of Persuasion

"It is not enough to instruct the lost and warn them of impending doom," writes Autrey, "... they must be persuaded."[12] Blackwood concurs that it is the preacher's aim "to bring his hearers face to face with the Son of God and persuade that hearer to accept Him as Savior and Lord."[13] Dr. Robert Dale has said, "To leave the truth to do its work, and to trust to the hearts and consciences of our hearers to apply it, is a great and fatal mistake."[14] J. I. Packer points out the aim of gospel communication:

> Evangelizing, therefore, is not simply a matter of teaching, and instructing, and imparting information to the mind. There is more to it than that. Evangelizing includes the endeavour to elicit a response to the truth taught. It is communication with a view to conversion. It is a matter, not merely of informing, but also of inviting. It is an attempt to *gain,* or *win,* or *catch,* our fellow-men for Christ.[15]

The Book of Acts contains several references to people being "persuaded" to believe in Christ (Acts 17:4; 18:4; 19:8,26; 28:23,24). The Apostle Paul wrote to the Corinthians, "Knowing therefore the terror of the Lord, we *persuade* men" (2 Corinthians 5:11 italics added). Jesus told the parable of the lord who instructed his servants to "Go out into the highways and hedges and *compel* them to come in, that my house may be filled" (Luke 14:23 italics added).

The invitation specifically attempts to *persuade* men to repent of their sins, trust in Christ to save them, and openly confess Him before men. To successfully persuade your people to appropriate the truth to their lives, you must be certain of four things. First, you must be sure yourself that Christ is the only way to salvation. Paul wrote to young Timothy, "I know whom I have believed, and am persuaded" (2 Timothy 1:12). Unless you are persuaded, you will be unable to persuade others. James H. Jauncey, a professional psychologist, remarks: "To be persuasive is to express enthusiastically a belief which we hold ourselves strongly."[16] Blackwood called it "a soul on fire."[17]

Second, you must make your invitation personal. The hearer needs to feel that you are speaking directly to him. No one will be persuaded if he feels you are speaking to his neighbor or the group as a whole. It is here that careful preparation is needed. Make sure your appeal includes many personal pronouns.

Third, you will want to fill your appeal with appropriate invitational Scriptures. This will take some research, but the results will be well worth the effort. God says through His prophet Isaiah, "So shall my word be that goeth forth out of my mouth: it shall not return unto me void, but it shall accomplish that which I please, and it shall prosper in the thing whereto I sent it" (Isaiah 55:11). Bishop Matthew Simpson writes:

> The preacher who quotes much of the Bible has, not only in the estimation of hearers the authority of "thus saith the Lord," but there is also a divine unseen power so joined to those words that they cannot be uttered without fruit.[18]

The biblical record is clear that the early disciples' success can be attributed to their use of God's Word: "Then they that gladly received his word were baptized" (Acts 2:41); "Many of them which heard the word believed; and the number of the men was about five thousand" (Acts 4:4); "And the word of God increased; and the number of disciples multiplied" (Acts 6:7).

The Word of God used by the Holy Spirit convicts men of their sins (Hebrews 4:12), enlightens their minds (Psalms 119:130), generates faith (Romans 10:17), and produces salvation (2 Timothy 3:15). As you freely quote God's Word, a divine power is released which can supernaturally persuade the listeners. Lewis A. Drummond explains the importance of using the Word:

> Because the gospel is the power of God we do not rely on human ingenuity, psychological manipulation, dramatics, or human invention to convince men of the truth and relevance of the message.
>
> God will speak for Himself through His Word. His Holy Spirit will press home the truth.[19]

Finally, you must be certain your invitation seeks to move the will of your hearer and bring it into submission to the Person of Jesus Christ. Your chief business is to obtain a favorable verdict on the spot, calling each individual in your audience to embrace the truth of the gospel and yield to Christ as Lord and Savior. The only reason man remains lòst in his sins is willful disobedience. He chooses to reject the claims, work, and Person of Jesus Christ. To the self-righteous Pharisees, Jesus said, "And ye *will not* come to me, that ye might have life" (John 5:40 italics added).

There are two avenues of approaching the will: the intellect and the emotions. A man can be moved to action if his mind can be convinced that the action is reasonable, and if his heart can be convinced that the action is necessary. You must, therefore, bring your hearer to the point where he says, "I can be saved (mind). I must be saved (emotions). I will be saved (will)." To achieve this result, you have first to present a logical argument why salvation is essential. Isaiah of old called out to his audience, "Come now, and let us *reason* together ... though your sins be as scarlet, they shall be as white as snow; though they be red like crimson, they shall be as wool" (Isaiah 1:18 italics added).

Next, you take aim on the heart. Intellectual acceptance of facts alone does not save. Men must be moved to take action. This is accomplished by speaking to their consciences. Logic has its place, but it must be set ablaze. Spurgeon advises: "A sinner has a heart as well as a head; a sinner has emotions as well as thoughts; and we must appeal to both. A sinner will never be converted until his emotions are stirred. Unless he feels sorrow for sin."[20]

Using a Motivational Theme

A highly effective method of reaching the will through the intellect and emotions is to use a motivating theme in each invitation. A topic of interest will help the hearer to see his need for salvation and lead him to make the appropriate response. A different theme should be developed for each invitation. This allows for freshness of material and furnishes the regular listener scores of reasons why he should come to Christ. People are moved to repent and believe on Christ for various reasons. Each theme will reach different members of the congregation. The following list is representative of the many motivating themes that can be effectively used:

Hope in the midst of a troubled world
A longing for truth
Escape from the consequences of sin
The danger of delay in coming to Christ
The fear of death
The longing to be loved
The possibility of forgiveness
Freedom from guilt; the burden of sin
A hungering for fulfillment
The possibility of a happy home
The guarantee of eternal life
Escape from boredom and loneliness
The desire to find rest
Help for personal problems
The rewards of heaven

You should select a motivating theme for each invitation. Let us say you choose, for example, the danger of delaying a decision for Christ. You have already completed developing a transitional statement and drafting instructions about the necessity of repenting, trusting, and confessing so that the people will clearly understand what is expected of them. Now, through the motivating theme, you will attempt to move them to the appropriate action.

First, you need to find Scripture passages that deal with the topic of delaying one's salvation. Verses such as the following can be used to show people that God calls them to be saved immediately: "Behold, now is the accepted time; behold, now is the day of salvation" (2 Corinthians 6:2); "Today if ye will hear his voice, harden not your hearts" (Hebrews 3:7,8); "Seek ye the LORD while he may be found, call ye upon him while He is near" (Isaiah 55:6).

Plan to intersperse these Scriptures with fitting exhortations aimed at moving people to apply these truths personally to their lives. You might exhort:

> God calls you today to respond to His offer of salvation
> ... not tomorrow, next week, or next year.... The Bible
> doesn't promise a second chance. Nowhere does it say,
> "Tomorrow is the day of salvation." ... God's invitation
> is always in the present tense. You need to come now!

From the Scriptures and accompanying exhortations, your listeners will clearly understand that God offers them salvation instantly, if they will only respond.

Next, you must plan an approach that will reach into the people's hearts and move them to act upon the truth. You might choose to emphasize the eternal consequence of delaying a decision for Christ. Again, you will want to select appropriate Scriptures: "He, that being often reproved hardeneth his neck, shall suddenly be destroyed, and that without remedy" (Proverbs 29:1); "The LORD said, My Spirit shall not always strive with man" (Genesis 6:3); "How shall we escape, if we neglect so great salvation?" (Hebrews 2:3); "Boast not thyself of tomorrow, for thou knowest not what a day may bring forth" (Proverbs 27:1). You should again prepare to exhort your people in between the verses:

> God's offer of salvation may not be made to you tomor-
> row. He may stop drawing you to Christ. Then it will be
> too late. You must decide now. Don't put it off another
> moment. When God issues a warning, you must respond
> or face the consequences. It is a serious matter to reject the
> offer of God. Life is short. None of us knows when the end

> may come. You may not be here tomorrow. Life may have
> ended for you. Or you may lose your reasoning abilities
> and be unable to make a decision for Christ. That's why
> God calls you now.

You may plan to include among the Scriptures and exhortations an effective illustration to drive the truth into the hearts of your listeners. This may be an illustration from the pages of the Bible, such as the parable of the rich fool who planned to build new barns to hoard his grain, to whom God said, "Thou fool, *this night* thy soul shall be required of thee" (Luke 12:16–21). Or you may choose to highlight the exhortation with an illustration from contemporary life. News events remain fresh in people's minds for weeks. The observant gospel preacher will make use of current events in order to win his people to Christ. The illustration need not be long. It just has to be effective. It must speak to hearts.

The first set of Scriptures and exhortations should be designed to reach the minds of the listeners. The second set should touch their feelings. These two steps make up the motivating theme, prepared for the purpose of ultimately reaching people's wills. But you must not conclude your preparation at this point. There is one more step to be taken.

The Call to Public Commitment

The most important aspect of the invitation is at hand. You must plan to issue an effective call for people to *act* upon the truth. If you fail here, the rest of your preparation is useless. The key to a successful invitation is persuading people to come to Christ.

Emotions can be aroused and the intellect stirred, but unless the sinner is challenged to exercise his will and given the opportunity to do so, it is unlikely he will do it on his own. This is why the public invitation is the hub of the evangelistic sermon.

You should carefully choose the method of public invitation you plan to use. (Chapter 9 discusses several of the more popular styles of invitations that have been used by God to bring people to His Son.) You might decide, for example, simply to call people forward during an invitational hymn. Several other factors may need to be considered. Will the choir sing alone? Do you want the people sitting or standing at this time? Should they have their heads bowed? Through experimentation you will soon learn what best fits your situation. Every detail of the call forward should be planned: from the music to who will greet the people when they come forward.

You will also need to prepare the content of your appeal. In doing this, you will want to keep several things in mind. First, plan to keep this portion of the invitation *simple:*

> As the choir begins to sing, I am going to ask you to get up out of your seat and come to the front of the auditorium. This will be your way of saying, "I want to receive Jesus Christ as my Savior. I want to repent and receive Him into my life today."

Make arrangements with the choir beforehand as to when they should begin singing during the invitation.

Next, plan to keep your appeal *personal.* You can do this by stating in various ways that God is no respecter of persons:

> Regardless of your position in life *you* need to come. *You* may be in school, employed fulltime, or be retired. *You* may be unemployed or a housewife. God calls *you* to make your commitment today. *You* may be black or white or oriental; God loves *you* and wants to give *you* eternal life. But *you* must come. He won't force it on *you.*

Always plan to issue a positive appeal, without apology. The pastor who opens his altar call with the words, "I know it is twelve o'clock, but I feel God would have me give an appeal for you to come to Christ" is undermining his office. The preacher owes no apology. You not only have a right to issue the call, but a divine obligation. As Spurgeon wrote: "Ambassadors do not apologize when they go to a foreign court; they know that their monarch has sent them, and they deliver their message with all the authority of king and country at their back."[21] With this authority in your possession, plan to address your listeners as if you were sent by God Himself to issue the call (2 Corinthians 5:20):

> *God* has spoken to you tonight. You have heard *His* voice. *He* is calling you. *He* is saying, "Come. Don't put off this decision again. I love you and want to forgive you." *God* may never speak to you again as *He* has tonight. You get up and come. We'll wait for you.

Time is a vital consideration. A general rule of thumb is, "The shorter, the better." You will have already instructed your people what it means to repent and believe. You will have also motivated them to act through the motivational theme. You must not allow your call to drag. People's hearts will have been touched. They will be ready to make their move. Therefore, plan to keep your appeal for action less than two minutes in length. Brevity is essential.

Finally, you should be prepared enough to deliver your invitation without the use of notes. If you are unable to memorize the entire invitation from the transition statement onward, at least memorize your final two-minute call. This will enable you to keep eye contact with your audience, so very important in the persuasion process.

How You Can Deliver an Effective Invitation

The day arrives for you to deliver your sermon. Your preparation is behind you; your efforts have been saturated with prayer. Confident that the Holy Spirit has guided you thus far, you are ready to preach the message God has laid on your heart. Whatever your general topic may be, your message ultimately brings the listeners to the foot of the cross where the Savior bled and died as a payment for sin. You make your transition from the main body of the sermon into the conclusion. The hard work and hours of preparation have paid off. After instructing your hearers, you now face the biggest challenge. You must persuade and call them to surrender willfully to Christ. This is the crucial point, the climax. If you, the herald, effectively deliver your exhortation and closing appeal, it is likely that lost people will find salvation. If you fail at this task, the results will be less than satisfactory. The destiny of men's souls hangs in the balance.

Voice Quality

Although you have thoroughly prepared yourself for this moment, actual delivery of the final appeal will not be easy. Be sure to keep three rules in mind as you begin the call. First, speak in a natural voice. This is no time to preach. Your tone must be conversational. You will not be addressing the crowd as a whole, but speaking to individuals. You may even choose a few people at random in the audience and speak directly to them.

End your sermon quietly, with what John Henry Jowett has called the "wooing note."[22] Seldom are people shouted into the kingdom. Dr. Blackwood urged his students at Princeton Theological Seminary:

> In the last few words of a message from the pulpit God speaks to the waiting soul, not "through the earthquake, wind, and fire," but through "the voice of gentle stillness." In wooing a maiden a young man does not try to carry a citadel by storm, but with quiet intensity presses his

claims, pleading that he loves her and wishes her above all else on earth.[23]

Christ woos His bride through the quiet appeal of the preacher.

Second, be sure you extend the invitation in a serious and earnest manner. With the eternal destiny of human beings at stake, you must not speak in a frivolous tone. The invitation is no place for introducing humor or levity. People must be made to realize, through your demeanor and quality of voice, that you are concerned about their spiritual welfare. Spurgeon listed earnestness as the most important factor in winning men to Christ.[24]

Third, pace your delivery. Do not rush through the invitation. Hurrying the appeal usually leads to mistakes in grammar and loss of thought, and could render the invitation ineffective. Carefully weigh your words and precisely deliver them.

Other Characteristics of Delivering an Effective Appeal

Several other rules should be followed if your invitation is to be effective. One is being careful not to distract your audience with unnecessary movements. Such actions as looking at your watch, wiping your brow with a handkerchief, reaching for the bulletin, closing the Bible, taking off your glasses, picking up a hymn book, or buttoning your jacket divert people's attention away from the appeal and toward your mannerisms. The invitation should be a time for concentration.

You should stick to your prepared material. There is a tendency during the invitation for the preacher to introduce new material or interject an immediate thought. To do so would be a mistake. If you are convinced the Holy Spirit guided your preparation, you should have confidence to follow your prearranged appeal. New ideas are out of place.

Another important rule to observe is to wait patiently for

people to respond after the final call has been given. At this juncture, you must turn the results over to the Holy Spirit. Resist the temptation to coax, to make numerous additional exhortations, or even to manipulate people into taking action. These pressure tactics are often used by preachers who are afraid no one will respond to their invitation. A fear of embarrassment and failure has caused many otherwise honest men of God to use trickery in obtaining results.

Hal Holbrook's one-man play on the life of Abraham Lincoln is a classic. In one scene he portrays Lincoln as a young, ambitious lawyer who decides to attend a revival service. At the conclusion of his message, the visiting evangelist issues the appeal, "All who want to go to heaven, stand immediately." A number of people respond. He then issues a second appeal, "All who want to go to hell, remain seated." This moves the remainder of the congregation to action, except for Abraham Lincoln. Wanting to assure complete success, the preacher addresses his lone rebel, "And Mr. Lincoln, where do you want to go?" To which Lincoln responds, "Congress, sir!"

The pastor or evangelist who resorts to chicanery deserves such a response. At all costs, maintain your integrity! You are representing the Lord Jesus Christ. If there is no immediate response to the invitation, don't panic; instead, begin praying. A spiritual battle is raging: Satan is doing everything in his power to keep people from surrendering to Christ. Heaven and hell are contending for men's eternal souls. You are in direct conflict with the forces of evil (Ephesians 6:12). Your only line of defense and hope of success is dependence on God. Paul writes, "For the weapons of our warfare are not carnal, but mighty through God to the pulling down of strongholds" (2 Corinthians 10:4).

Silent prayer following the final appeal often spells the difference between success and failure. Finney said, "Work as if everything depended upon us, and pray as if everything depended on God."[25] Commenting on the importance of prayer during the invitation, Spurgeon advised, "Prayer and means go together. Means without prayer—presumption. Prayer without means—hypocrisy."[26]

Billy Graham tells of the events surrounding his invitation on the first night of his All-Scotland Crusade. For weeks he was advised not to issue a public invitation. Public calls to commitment were not part of the church's tradition in Scotland. Graham was warned that even if he did issue an appeal, no one would respond. Despite the numerous admonitions, he gave his usual call for people to come forward. He tells the story as it happened:

> Then came the moment of decision. Would they come? Would they respond?
> I asked them to bow their heads, and then quietly gave the invitation. At first not a person moved. My heart began to sink a little. My faith wavered only for a second, and then it all came flooding back to me that millions of people were praying and that God was going to answer their prayers. Then great faith came surging into my heart, and I knew they would come even before I saw the first one move. I bowed my head and began to pray. Then I glanced up and people were streaming from everywhere. I saw some of the ministers with their clerical collars, on the platform, begin to weep.[27]

After fervently praying, you must be ready to accept God's results. Wait patiently until the people stop responding. If there is little or no response, you should wait only a minute or two before closing the meeting. Autrey gives good theological advice: "The soul-winner must respect the rights of others, even the right to die in their sins if they persist."[28]

If you are diligent in your preparation and careful to execute your delivery properly, depending totally on God, you will experience many more successes than failures in your attempts to win people to Christ.

9

Invitational Models

Evangelistic invitations fall into two major categories: those which call upon sinners to make an immediate decision for Christ, and those which call for a delayed response. Invitations in each classification have been successfully used to lead people to Christ. All have certain advantages and disadvantages inherent in their nature. Unfortunately, some invitational methods have been used abusively. It is advisable, therefore, that evangelistic preachers use great skill and tact in issuing a public invitation. The wrong handling of the invitation can do irreparable damage to the cause of evangelism.

Because of the wide variety of invitational styles, each pastor or evangelist must discover for himself the model which best fits his personality, theological interests, and church setting. The minister of the gospel may have to experiment with different methods. Through trial and error, he will discern what type of invitation best suits his particular needs. He may choose to use only one method or he may decide that several of the models will be serviceable.

Different models can be adapted to different circumstances. Some invitational methods are conducive to a small church setting, while others are more adaptable to the large evangelistic campaign. A call for people to come forward, for example, is not always appropriate or even practical. Setting up a private appointment with the pastor or guest evangelist may be more advantageous in many instances.

The Delayed-Response Invitation

The delayed-response invitation challenges listeners to ponder the content of the gospel, and then decide if they desire to become Christians. If the decision is affirmative, they then meet with the preacher at a designated time and location. There are several methods of public invitation which fall into this category.

The After Meeting

The after meeting takes place ten or fifteen minutes after the close of the worship or evangelistic service. At the end of his sermon, the preacher invites those in his audience who are interested in becoming Christians, or who are interested in knowing more about the Christian faith, to meet with him in another room. The after meeting begins promptly with an opening prayer. The preacher explains to those in attendance the plan of salvation. He urges them to surrender fully to Christ, and gives them an opportunity to do so immediately. He may ask them to raise their hands, stand, sign a card, come forward, or express their desire to receive Christ by some other indication. Those who so indicate are counseled by a personal worker.

The after meeting was the invitational method used by Asahel Nettleton and several other prominent evangelists since his time. On occasion, when practical circumstances call for it, Billy Graham will make use of the after meeting. During one trip to England, for instance, Graham used this method after addressing the student body at Cambridge University.[1]

Dr. Leroy Patterson, chaplain at Wheaton College, frequently closes his services with a short period of silent prayer, followed by an invitation for those whom the Lord has touched through the message to meet with him in his study. Following the benediction, he goes directly to his study where he prays and waits.[2]

There are several advantages in using an after meeting. First, it eliminates undue pressure on people to make an "immediate" decision for Christ. They have a few minutes to deliberate. Second, it eliminates the embarrassment often associated with walking forward or other types of public invitations. Third, the after meeting eliminates the dramatic element and circus atmosphere of the call to Christ. Next, it separates the sincere seekers from the curiosity seekers. Finally, it offers a quiet place apart where the pastor can speak in private to the inquirers.

Special Appointments

Another type of delayed-response invitation is the special appointment method. At the close of his sermon, the preacher invites those in his congregation who are concerned about their relationship with God to call the church office to set up a private meeting with the pastor. Since people are used to setting up appointments for all kinds of things from dental appointments to hair appointments, this method is an acceptable practice for most people.

The main advantage of this method is that it permits the seeker and the pastor to choose a mutually convenient meeting time. The appointment can be worked into a busy schedule. Second, this method shows the inquirer that the preacher is concerned about him as a person, not as a statistic. Finally, it allows for total privacy in dealing with the seeker's spiritual needs.

The Signing of Cards

Some evangelistic preachers are more comfortable in having inquirer's cards placed in each pew. Those anxious about their soul's salvation are urged at the close of the gospel message to fill in a card, including name, address, and telephone number. The card is then given to the preacher or usher at the end of the meeting. All persons who turn in a card receive a visit from the minister at a later date to discuss their spiritual need. This method was used by B. Fay Mills in the early 1900s. Campus Crusade for Christ presently utilizes this method in an effective way.

The key advantage of this style of invitation is that it enables seekers to meet with the preacher in the comfort and privacy of their own home. In familiar surroundings, seekers are at ease and more likely to open their hearts to the minister. With distractions eliminated, counseling can be done more effectively than at an altar or in a noisy room.

Special Classes

Another form of the delayed-response invitation is the special class method. At the conclusion of his sermon, the preacher makes an announcement that a class will be started the following week for those interested in learning more about the Christian faith. Patterson relates:

> The first time I issued this kind of an invitation I was totally unprepared for the results. I had 18 people respond, and after six months I ended with 32. Most of these were people who were uncommitted but definitely interested. From that class came a number of very positive, intelligent decisions for Christ. I am confident that few of these would have responded to an altar call but they were seekers.[3]

The special class method is beneficial because it allows time for a relationship to be established between the inquirers and the minister. Another asset these sessions guarantee is that the instruction will be thorough. It also presents numerous opportunities for valuable interchange between the students and the teacher.

The Delayed Altar Call

The preacher who uses this method announces, at the end of his gospel message, that an altar call will be given the following week. In the meantime, the people are to go home and think about their need to receive Christ. They should return the next week prepared to make a public commitment.

Because of the time element involved, the Holy Spirit is given a full week to convict the hearts of sinners. He is not forced to work in a few minutes' time, as He is under some other methods. Additionally, the delayed altar call is valuable in that it psychologically prepares the people for the public invitation. They know what to expect. They are not caught off guard; they do not feel pressured.

The Dangers of the Delayed-Response Invitation

All delayed-response invitational methods have their disadvantages as well as their advantages. The most serious defect is that God calls sinners to be saved immediately, not fifteen minutes later, three days later or one week later. "*Now* is the accepted time; behold, *now* is the day of salvation" (2 Corinthians 6:2 italics added). Jesus said, "Repent: for the kingdom of heaven is *at hand*" (Matthew 4:17). The gospel writer Mark records that Jesus' disciples left their nets and followed Him "*straightway*" (Mark 1:16–20). They were obedient. When Jesus called, He expected decisions to be made without delay (*see* Matthew 8:21,22).

On October 8, 1871, Dwight L. Moody learned the hard way the danger of giving sinners time "to think it over" before coming to Christ. On that date he preached on the text, "What then shall I do with Jesus which is called Christ?" After completing his sermon, he said to the audience, "I wish you would take this text home with you and turn it over in your minds during the week, and next Sabbath we will come to Calvary and the cross, and we will decide what to do with Jesus of Nazareth."[4]

Instead of calling for an immediate commitment, he gave the members of the congregation a week to think about it. Tragically, many did not live to see the break of day, must less another week. The very moment Moody was closing his sermon, the great Chicago fire was beginning to rage out of control. Entire city blocks were destroyed, killing hundreds and leaving ninety thousand people homeless. Moody sadly recalled the event:

> What a mistake! I have never dared to give an audience a week to think of their salvation since. If they were lost they might rise up in judgment against me. I remember Mr. Sankey singing, and how his voice rang when he came to that pleading verse:
>
> > Today the Savior calls,
> > For refuge fly!
> > The storm of Justice falls,
> > And death is nigh!
>
> I have never seen that congregation since. I have hard work to keep back the tears today. . . . But I want to tell you of one lesson I learned that night, which I have never forgotten, and that is, when I preach, to press Christ upon the people then and there, and try to bring them to a decision on the spot. I would rather have that right hand cut off than to give an audience now a week to decide what to do with Jesus.[5]

The mistake Moody made that evening he would later call the greatest blunder of his ministry.[6] Delay often pays spiritual dividends that are devastating.

The second negative aspect of a delayed-response invitation is that it allows the convicted person an opportunity to quench the voice of the Holy Spirit. The Spirit of God speaks through the Word of God to produce faith and draw men to Christ. People are more likely to receive Christ as Savior if the invitation comes while they are under conviction. Any delay may give sinners time to get their minds off the issues at hand and become occupied with the things of the world. Although the Spirit may still be speaking, they are not sensitive to His voice. An act as simple as congregating with friends after an evangelistic meeting and talking over harmless items of interest can be enough to make the lost person lose his sense of need. Conviction will have been dampened; no longer can he hear the Spirit speaking to his heart.

Dr. D. Martyn Lloyd-Jones tells of an experience he had some years ago. One Sunday evening as he was delivering his sermon he noticed a man weeping in the audience. Although Lloyd-Jones sensed an urge to speak to the man about his soul at the close of the sermon, he held his peace. The following evening, the preacher happened to meet this same man along the roadway. Lloyd-Jones continues the story:

> He came across the road to me and said, "You know, doctor, if you had asked me to stay behind last night I would have done so." "Well," I said, "I am asking you now, come with me now." "Oh no," he replied, "but if you had asked me last night I would have done so."[7]

A third negative of the delayed-response invitation is that it gives Satan an opportunity to snatch away the Word which has been placed in the sinner's heart. In His parable of the sower and the four soils, Jesus describes some seed as falling "by the wayside" (Luke 8:5). In explaining the meaning of this parable, Jesus said, "Now the parable is this: The seed is the word of

God. Those by the wayside are they that hear; then cometh the devil, and taketh away the word out of their hearts, lest they should believe and be saved" (Luke 8:11,12).

Satan does everything in his power to keep sinners from being saved. The delayed-response invitation allows him the time necessary to steal the Word of God from human hearts. With the Word removed, faith is impossible.

A final disadvantage in waiting to deal with a person about his salvation is that the Holy Spirit may not be drawing that person at a later date. The lost can only come to Christ when they are being drawn (John 6:44). For this reason, when a sinner hears the voice of God speaking to his heart, that is the time to respond. Delay may mean missing an opportunity to be saved (Matthew 25:10–12).

When the Holy Spirit moves in a powerful way during the preaching of the gospel, people are convicted of their sins and drawn to Christ. At these times, it is imperative that the minister extend an invitation (Revelation 22:17). Neglect to do so in these moments could mean that many in the audience will miss being reconciled with God. Pastors and evangelists must preach as dying men to dying men; as if each sermon is the last they will ever preach, and the last sermon their congregation will ever hear.

Although certain disadvantages built into the delayed-response invitation cannot be remedied, it would be a mistake never to use this method. There are situations where the delayed-response method is the only feasible alternative. Better to issue this kind of invitation than none at all!

The Immediate-Response Invitation

Any invitation that calls upon unbelievers to repent and trust in Christ, and gives them an immediate opportunity to do so, is an immediate-response invitation. In this category we shall examine several models.

The Altar Call

What has popularly become known as the altar call is an invitation made by the preacher at the conclusion of his sermon for sinners immediately to leave their seats and come to the front of the auditorium. This physical act outwardly indicates the respondent's desire to turn from sin and to Christ. This method has been used effectively by Billy Sunday, Billy Graham, and a myriad of other evangelists during the twentieth century.

Those who respond to the invitation may kneel at an altar or be met by the minister as they come forward. W. A. Criswell greets his inquirers with a handshake and a word of encouragement. He then introduces them to the congregation.[8]

The advantages of the altar call are twofold. First, it calls for an immediate decision. No delay is involved. People are asked to respond while the Holy Spirit is ministering to their hearts. Second, the act of public profession motivates the new believer to confess Christ to others in the future. The initial fear of testifying publicly is eliminated. The altar call method helps the convert to witness boldly. His decision for Christ has not been made secretly; neither will his Christian lifestyle be hidden from view.

The Raising of Hands and Standing at the Seat

Rather than call people forward, some preachers of the gospel prefer to ask sinners to respond publicly in their seats. The usual procedure is for the minister at the close of his sermon to ask everyone to bow his head for prayer. He then invites those who wish to be saved to so indicate by raising their hands or standing at their seats. The preacher prays for their welfare and concludes by asking the seekers to repeat audibly the sinner's prayer after him.

The main benefit of this method is it can be used in situations where it is impossible to call people forward, while still affording them an opportunity to make an immediate and public stand for Christ.

The Act of Public Confession

Another significant immediate-response invitation is the act of public confession. This differs from the other styles because it does not invite people to receive Christ as Savior publicly. After preaching the gospel message, the evangelist asks all persons present to bow their heads and close their eyes. He then invites those who wish to receive Christ to repeat a sinner's prayer silently after him. Since everything has been done with eyes closed, silently, and without any physical movement, those who pray to be saved remain anonymous. After the prayer is completed, the preacher calls for all who followed his instructions to stand or come forward. This public act is the new converts' first opportunity to confess Christ openly and unashamedly.

Many preachers choose this method of invitation because it permits sinners to be saved privately. People are not pressured to come forward or take any public action to be saved. While new believers are encouraged to follow their decision for Christ with a public confession of faith, the pressure is again eliminated since no one knows who the new converts are until they respond.

The Progressive Invitation

The purpose of the progressive invitation is to use easy progressive steps in leading people to a salvation experience. The evangelistic preacher begins his invitation by asking those who want prayer for salvation to raise their hands. Those who respond are then asked to either stand or come forward so the preacher can pray for them. Other preliminary steps may precede the call forward, but the progression always concludes with an attempt to move the seeker to the front of the auditorium.

The progressive method is possibly the weakest of the immediate-response invitations. It calls upon people to take successive steps they originally never planned to take. Some people would not raise their hands for prayer if they knew they were also going to be called upon to stand or go forward. Once they make an initial public response, they often feel trapped into following the other instructions. Embarrassment is usually the end result.

Despite its weaknesses, the progressive invitation, in the hands of a skillful and sensitive preacher, does have a favorable quality. Some people need to be led to Christ one step at a time. Each successive step brings them closer to a full surrender to Christ.

Baptism

Baptism has been used effectively throughout church history as an act of public commitment. Peter called upon his listeners to "Repent and be baptized every one of you" (Acts 2:38). All Baptist and most independent Bible churches consider baptism to be the initial act of public confession after one becomes a Christian. For this reason some pastors and evangelists issue two invitations at the conclusion of their gospel messages: one for salvation and one for believer's baptism.

Over the years, many ministers have also noticed "that the services which open with the ordinance of baptism are the services most likely to close with visible responses to the evangelistic invitation."[9] This interesting observation may speak of the importance of baptism as an instrument in the evangelistic process. Since the ordinance of baptism is a picture of the gospel, declaring forth the death, burial, and resurrection of Jesus Christ, it reinforces the gospel sermon which follows. Also, people are present for a baptismal service who do not normally attend church services. Unsaved relatives and friends, as a result of attending the baptism, come under the preaching of the evangel and are converted.

The Private Decision

Using this method, the preacher at the conclusion of his sermon asks his congregation to bow for prayer. He then challenges those who want to be saved to repeat silently a sinner's prayer after him. Rather than call the new believers forward, the minister invites them to let him know of their commitment to Christ before they leave the building. Dr. C. Sumner Wemp relates his use of this method:

> I ask people to pray in their hearts right where they are and make the decision the Holy Spirit is prompting them to make. Then to let me know they have and as indication of the definiteness of the decision, I ask them to look up at me and catch my eye and in so doing to say by that they have made the decision and are sure of it.[10]

The main advantage of the private decision method is that it is immediate, but does not pressure people to make a public indication at this time. Their desire to tell the preacher of their commitment signifies their sincerity.

The Dangers of the Immediate-Response Invitation

All forms of the immediate-response invitation have flaws. No method of inviting people to Christ is without its disadvantages.

Those forms of the immediate-response invitation which call people forward or to make some visible indication of their faith are susceptible to gimmickry. Some preachers feel their success is measured solely by the number of people who respond to the public invitation. This attitude often leads them to use unethical means to gain "converts."

Another drawback of the immediate-response invitation is the tendency to number all inquirers as converts. Blackwood said the public invitation frequently induces unconverted people to profess faith in Christ.[11] Commenting on this danger, Spurgeon said:

> You may say to yourself, at the close of a service, "Here is a splendid haul of fish!" Wait a bit. Remember our Savior's words, "The kingdom of heaven is like a net, that was cast into the sea, and gathered of every kind; which, when it was full, they drew to the shore, and sat down, and gathered the good into vessels, but cast the bad away." Do not number your fishes before they are broiled; nor count your converts before you have tested and tried them.[12]

Counting all who publicly respond to an invitation as truly converted can backfire. Stewart remarks, "Remember, an empty profession is no triumph for the gospel. An empty profession brings no glory to God. An empty profession brings incalculable harm to the evangelical cause."[13]

The final weakness of many immediate-response invitations is the lack of follow-through counseling. If sinners are called upon to pray silently, raise their hands, stand to their feet, or even come forward, and then receive little or no counseling, their commitment may be short-lived.

John Dillinger, declared "public enemy number one" by the FBI, was the most ruthless and notorious gangster of the 1930s. As a teenager, Dillinger attended Sunday School. A documented article relates the story:

> In a little country church in Indiana there are some Sunday School records that have John Dillinger's name on them. Young John Dillinger went to Sunday School for

seven Sundays, then he missed. Then he went, then he missed and missed. Finally, by the name of John Dillinger is written: "Dropped."[14]

Why was Dillinger a Sunday School dropout? An article from Rex Humbard's *Answer* magazine provides the surprising answer:

> Back in 1942 we were in Cadle Tabernacle at Indianapolis. A lady came up to me after I had prayed with many young people that night. We had over 8,000 there and when I gave the invitation many hundreds came forward for prayer.
> As I was getting ready to leave this nice looking lady took me by the hand and said, "Rex, you don't know me, but I want to thank you for praying with those young people. Years ago my brother got into trouble in our community. People there told their children, 'Don't have anything to do with John, because he's a bad boy.' We had a meeting in a country church and one night during that meeting John's heart was moved. He got up out of his seat and came down to the altar. But because no one came to pray with him, in just a few moments John got up and walked to the back of the church. He looked at me and said, 'I'm never going into another church again.' He didn't. My brother's name was John Dillinger."
> Tears welled up in that woman's eyes as she told me her story. I remembered reading about Dillinger. He had used the powers of his life to glorify evil. Years ago his heart was tender, but he turned from God that night.[15]

Certainly Dillinger was morally responsible for his actions, but the fact that no one counseled with him after he responded to a public invitation must be considered a contributing factor. According to his own testimony, it was this oversight that turned him away from God. This tragic story shows why the immediate-response invitation must be accompanied by thorough counseling if it is to be used in an effective and responsible manner.

The Importance of Counseling

Early in his ministry Billy Graham came to recognize the need for an effective counseling program. Originally, Graham did not use counselors or personal workers, but simply addressed the mass of seekers himself. Conservation of the decisions was left in the hands of local pastors. When Graham noticed that many of the new believers were falling by the wayside, he concluded that a follow-up program must be established. He called on his friend Dawson Trotman, founder of The Navigators, to establish the most extensive mass evangelistic counseling ministry ever developed in church history.

All pastors and evangelists need to realize the importance of counseling with inquirers and following through with them until maturity is developed. Personal counseling can be effectively accomplished in one of two ways. The first is to use personal workers during invitation time. The second is to use an inquiry room.

The Ministry of Personal Workers

As the preacher extends the invitation, personal workers should be scattered throughout the congregation. They will be on the lookout for two things. First, they should be watching for those people who respond by standing, raising their hands, going forward, or whatever the invitation calls them to do. The personal workers will immediately pair themselves off with seekers, one personal worker for every seeker if possible. Each personal worker is then responsible to thoroughly counsel the inquirer until the latter has peace with God and assurance of salvation (Romans 5:1; 1 John 5:13). Information such as name, address, telephone number, church affiliation, and age of the convert should be obtained and passed on to the pastor or evangelist.

Second, as the invitation is extended, personal workers should be on the lookout for those who do not respond publicly but appear to be under conviction of sin. When such a person is spotted, a personal worker should cautiously and inconspicuously approach the individual and gently exhort him to make his commitment to Christ. When the invitation calls for sinners to walk forward, the personal worker may say, "I'll be happy to go with you, if you want." These words of encouragement can be used of God to save a soul. Jerry Falwell, pastor of the Thomas Road Baptist Church in Lynchburg, Virginia, tells how a personal worker was instrumental in leading him to Christ. As an eighteen-year-old college sophomore seeking for God, he attended a small Baptist church in his hometown. He relates:

> And that night, when the invitation was given, I didn't know what to do. An old white-haired man behind me knew I was a lost ball in the high weeds, and put his hand on my shoulder and said, "Son, would you like to go down there and accept Christ?" I said, "More than anything else."
> "Would you like me to go with you?"
> I said I surely would. He was God's man on the spot.
> I didn't own a Bible, didn't know a verse of Scripture but when I walked out of that building that night, January 20, 1952, my whole life was turned around and nothing has been the same since.[16]

Doing personal work during the invitation is a very delicate task. If improperly handled, it can drive as many people away from Christ as it brings to Christ. Every personal worker should have a direct leading from God before approaching a convicted sinner. He should also possess the gift of exhortation. (The early Methodist Church had such "exhorters" who were specially gifted in leading people to Christ during the invitation; *see* Chapter 4.) Finally, if the convicted individual refuses the exhortation, the personal worker should graciously retreat without pressuring the sinner any further.

The Inquiry Room

The inquiry room is best used in conjunction with the altar call style of invitation. All concerned inquirers who respond to the invitation by coming forward are ushered into an adjacent room where personal workers counsel with each on an individual basis. This method of counseling was introduced by Dwight L. Moody at the close of the nineteenth century[17] and has been effectively used by many pastors and evangelists since.

The inquiry room allows the counselor to deal with the inquirer in a relatively quiet setting, free from noisy distractions and unwelcome interruptions. The purpose of the counseling session is to help the inquirer to solidify his decision for Christ and to instruct him how to grow in the faith. An information card can be filled out and turned over to the follow-up chairman. Also, a supply of helpful literature can be housed in the inquiry room to hand out to the new believer.

All invitational models have both positive and negative features. The good points far outweigh the flaws. The few problems that do exist should not cause the evangelistic preacher to stop issuing invitations. Any type of appeal that affords the sinner an opportunity to repent and believe on Christ is better than no appeal at all.

The immediate-response invitation is closer to the New Testament pattern than the delayed-response model because it calls upon sinners to make an instantaneous decision for Christ. Any on-the-spot commitment to Christ must be accompanied by extensive counseling. And every new convert should be discipled in the faith following his salvation experience.

10

Music and the Invitation

What effect does music, during the worship or evangelistic service, have on drawing people to Christ at invitation time? Apparently the Apostle Paul believed music to be an important instrument in soul winning. Although Scripture does not reveal what songs Paul and Silas sang during their imprisonment at Philippi (Acts 16:25), it does record the amazing results of their singing. The jailer cried out, "Sirs, what must I do to be saved?" (Acts 16:30). Donald P. Ellsworth comments:

> Unquestionably the jailer was moved to ask this question partly because of the great earthquake which they had just experienced. However, there is nothing intrinsic in an earthquake which would encourage a man to seek to be saved. Paul's and Silas's singing must have had something to do with it. We can be reasonably sure that the songs were at least meaningful to those prisoners who were listening, because Paul writes elsewhere (1 Corinthians 14:15) that singing is to be done with the understanding.[1]

When used evangelistically, music has a strong influence in bringing people to Christ. Paul said he used "all means" to win men to Christ (1 Corinthians 9:22). Music certainly falls into this category.

How Music Has Been Used to Win Souls

Music has been used in evangelism throughout history. James Sallee remarks, "Every great religious movement has been accompanied by songs."[2]

John Chrysostom, the greatest gospel preacher of the fourth century, often marched through the streets singing psalms to the glory of God.[3] Many onlookers would join the procession that led to the steps of the church. John "the golden-mouthed" would then preach an evangelistic message.

In this same era, Niceta of Remesiana "spread the gospel among fourth-century pagans in southeastern Europe by singing songs whose themes centered on the Cross."[4]

During the Dark and Middle Ages, music was silenced by the Roman Catholic Church. Only clergy were allowed to sing. On those rare occasions when the laity were permitted to sing, they had to address their singing to the Virgin Mary or the saints.

Francis of Assisi (1182–1226), considered a fanatic and renegade by the Roman Catholic hierarchy, effectively used music to win men to Christ. Francis' psalms, hymns, and spiritual songs attracted many people to Christ[5] and earned him the title, "Troubadour of God."

It was not until the advent of the Protestant Reformation in the sixteenth century that music gained widespread popularity among the masses. The reformers wrote scriptural songs— usually the Psalms put to music—in order to put the Word of God into the hands of the people. Martin Luther, the leading figure of the Reformation, was a prolific song writer. By the mid-1600s, many of his metrical psalms were being used as congregational hymns in Protestant churches throughout Europe. The Roman Catholic Church feared Luther's hymns as much as his doctrine. George Stansbury says that Luther's songs were used by God to propagate the Christian faith and that "great masses of people with his melodies on their lips sang themselves into the stream of the Protestant Reformation."[6] Edward Ninde states: "Cases are on record where whole towns were so moved that the people in a body went over to the new faith. No wonder that indignant Romanites declared that 'Luther's songs have damned more souls than all his books and speeches!' "[7]

Luther's music remained popular in Protestant circles throughout the seventeenth century. Some of his hymns are still used today.

The eighteenth century brought with it a mighty revival in America known as the Great Awakening. In 1734, through the preaching of Jonathan Edwards of Northampton, Massachusetts, and George Whitefield, British evangelist, the Holy Spirit moved in great force among the colonists. This fresh outpouring of the Spirit called for a fresh array of songs. Sallee remarks, "The slow and straightforward singing of the Psalms was not conducive to the revival spirit."[8] In addition, the musical psalms were basically Old Testament in theology. A new type of song was needed to accommodate Christian truth. Edwards and Whitefield turned to the hymns of Isaac Watts (1674–1748). According to Sallee, Watts almost singlehandedly transformed the psalm into the hymn.[9] Watts had three criteria for a hymn:[9]

1. It had to be evangelistic, filled with the light of the gospel.

2. It was freely composed, rather than an exact translation of Scripture.

3. It was written to express the thoughts and feelings of the singer.

Although Watts was Calvinistic in doctrine, some of his hymns included invitations for sinners to come to Christ. Under the heading "The Invitation of the Gospel," Watts penned these words:

> Let every mortal ear attend
> And every heart rejoice;
> The trumpet of the gospel sounds
> With an inviting voice.

The first verse of another Watts hymn entitled "Christ's Invitation to Sinners" went:

> Come hither all ye weary souls
> Ye heavy laden sinners, come,
> I'll give you rest from all your toils
> And raise you to my heavenly home.[10]

While America was in the midst of her spiritual renewal, Great Britain was also experiencing the fires of revival. The Wesley brothers, John and Charles, were evangelizing England through spoken word and song. John's gospel messages, which emphasized Christ's unlimited atonement and man's free will, accompanied by his brother's spirited hymns, resulted in thousands entering God's kingdom.

Charles Wesley (1707–1788), the writer of more than six thousand hymns, is credited with two major accomplishments. He was the first hymn writer to introduce a congregational style of singing that expressed the thoughts and feelings of the individual.[11]

Second, Wesley is credited with the writing of the first invitational hymns.[12] Several hundred of his hymns were written with one purpose in mind: to bring people to Christ.[13] At the end of each new sermon, John Wesley expected his brother to have a new invitational song ready. Donald P. Ellsworth includes the following untitled hymn among Wesley's invitational selections:

> Come, sinners, to the gospel feast;
> Let every soul be Jesus' guest;
> Ye need not one be left behind,
> For God hath bidden all mankind.
>
> This is the time; no more delay!
> This is the Lord's accepted day;
> Come thou, this moment, at His call,
> And live for Him who died for all.[14]

The Methodist Hymnal includes Charles Wesley's hymn, "Come, Let Us, Who in Christ Believe." Its third and fourth verses read:

> Thro' grace we harken to thy voice,
> Yield to be saved from sin;
> In sure and certain hope rejoice
> That thou wilt enter in.
>
> Come quickly in, thou heavenly guest,
> Nor ever hence remove;
> But sup with us, and let the feast
> Be everlasting love.[15]

The first verse of Wesley's "Jesus, the Sinner's Friend, to Thee" reads:

> Jesus, the sinner's friend, to thee,
> Lost and undone, for aid I flee,
> Weary of earth, myself and sin:
> Open thine arms, and take me in.

The tunes of Wesley's hymns were mostly borrowed from popular folk songs of his day, including some barroom ballads. Wesley's intentions were good. He believed the familiarity of the tunes would attract the lost masses of common people to listen to the hymn. The words could then be used by God to convict sinful hearts and turn them to Christ.

Charles Wesley's hymns were actually gospel sermons put to music. Ellsworth concludes that they did as much to bring men to Christ as John Wesley's sermons.[16]

Evangelistic music reached a new zenith in the early 1800s with the introduction of a new type of hymn called the "gospel song."[17] According to David Appleby, "The gospel song was born in the emotionally charged atmosphere of the camp meeting."[18] Its entire aim was "to reach people who possessed little or no education with the personal message of salvation in such a way as would be clearly understood by all."[19]

A unique characteristic of the gospel song was the inclusion of a chorus or refrain, which was repeated after each verse. Often the chorus took the form of an exhortation, warning, or invitation.

The gospel song gained popularity among the masses when it became the primary style of music used by the newly-founded Salvation Army, Young Men's Christian Association (YMCA), and the Sunday School Movement which was sweeping both America and Europe.

In the era of gospel songs, two men stand out as leaders. They are Philip P. Bliss (1838–1876) and Ira Sankey (1840–1908). Both were associated with Dwight L. Moody's evangelistic campaigns. In 1874 Moody published *Gospel Hymns,* a collection of fifty-two of Bliss' songs. The booklet was used in all of Moody's campaigns. Later, Sankey added his own gospel songs to form a new publication, *Sacred Songs and Solos.* It was so popular that for several years it was outsold only by the Bible.

Bliss' gospel song, "Free from the Law, O Happy Condition," is a perfect example of how this style of song called men to Christ. Its opening verse tells of the Savior's death which redeems man from the curse of the Law. The second verse and refrain read:

> Now are we free—there's no condemnation,
> Jesus provides a perfect salvation;
> "Come unto Me," O hear His sweet call,
> Come, and He saves us once for all.
>
> Once for all—O sinner, receive it;
> Once for all—O brother, believe it;
> Cling to the cross, the burden will fall,
> Christ hath redeemed us once for all.

Another of Bliss' gospel songs, "Whosoever Heareth, Shout, Shout" is taken from Revelation 22:17, "Whosoever will, let him take the water of life freely." Its second verse and refrain read:

> Whosoever cometh need not delay,
> Now the door is open, enter while you may;
> Jesus is the true, the only Living Way:
> "Whosoever will may come."
>
> Whosoever will, whosoever will!
> Send the proclamation over vale and hill;
> 'Tis a loving Father calls the wanderer home:
> "Whosoever will may come."[20]

In 1876 Bliss was killed in a tragic train accident. Upon hearing the sad news, Dwight L. Moody said:

> I believe he was raised up of God to write hymns for the Church of Christ in this age, as Charles Wesley was for the Church in his day. His songs have gone around the world, and have led, and will continue to lead, hundreds of souls to Christ.[21]

After the death of Bliss, Ira Sankey served as Moody's musician. Together they learned how to use music effectively in evangelism. Moody was particularly interested in music as an instrument in winning souls. He once wrote:

> I feel sure that the great majority of people do like singing. It helps to build up an audience—even if you preach a dry sermon. If you have singing that reaches the heart, it will fill the church every time. There is more said in the Bible about praise than prayer, and music and song have not only accompanied all scriptural revivals, but are essential in deepening spiritual life. Singing does at least as much as preaching to impress the Word of God upon people's minds.[22]

"Moody thought that a song which did not result in a response from the audience was not good music," said Sallee.[23] For this reason Sankey carefully chose to use only songs that presented the gospel, touched the heart, and invited men to Christ. His music was so persuasive in drawing men to the Savior that during the 1873 Great Britain campaign, the Reverend A. A. Rees, director of publicity, designed posters which read, "Moody will preach the gospel. Sankey will sing the gospel."[24]

Before Moody even rose to speak, his audience had been moved emotionally by the singing of Sankey. Scores of testimonies abound of people who were saved during the preliminary song service. At the conclusion of his message, as an aid to the invitation, Moody called upon his colleague to sing a solo invitational hymn.[25] Some of Sankey's favorites were "Only a Step to Jesus," "Only Trust Him," "Let the Savior In," "Why Not Tonight?", "Pass Me Not," Bliss' "Almost Persuaded," and "The Ninety and Nine," for which Sankey wrote the music. Sankey also made Charlotte Elliott's gospel song "Just As I Am" popular as an invitational hymn. In his autobiography, Ira Sankey relates numerous stories of people who attributed their salvation directly to the words of a gospel song.[26] Moody often remarked that fifty percent of the credit for his successful evangelistic efforts belonged to Ira Sankey.[27]

Moody and Sankey were pioneers in the concept of combining preaching with evangelistic music. They were the first evangelist and singer team in church history. Others would soon follow. One of the most noteworthy was composed of evangelist Reuben A. Torrey and Charles Alexander (1867–1920). Alexander, a graduate of Moody Bible Institute, also served for a few years with evangelist J. Wilbur Chapman.

Alexander was the forerunner of the modern-day song leader, combining musical talents with leadership abilities to serve as master of ceremonies for Dr. Torrey's evangelistic meetings.[28] Alexander believed in "warming up" an audience by involving the people in the service. He is also credited with forming the first massive, citywide choir which joined together to sing nightly during the services. His other major contribution to evangelistic music was to substitute the piano for the organ to accompany the singing. Up to that time, only organs had been used for that purpose.[29]

One reason Alexander devoted himself to a ministry of evangelistic music was personal: he had been saved while hearing Watts' hymn, "When I Survey the Wondrous Cross." He testified:

> I could not describe the feeling that came over me as they sang the third verse:
>
> > "See! from His head, His hands, His feet,
> > Sorrow and love flow mingled down!
> > Did e'er such love and sorrow meet,
> > Or thorns compose so rich a crown?"
>
> I got down and cried as I have never cried before nor since. The love of Christ did it. I stood when the invitation was given and went to the front.[30]

Alexander's great desire was to see others won to Christ through music. His many innovations were used by God to this end.

Another nationally-known evangelistic team was Billy Sunday and Homer Rodeheaver (1880–1955). Rodeheaver, a former college cheerleader, teamed up with Sunday in 1910. His background uniquely equipped him to enthusiastically lead the song service, which consisted of thirty minutes of lively congregational singing. Through various methods, Rodeheaver was able to involve the audience in the service. He recruited church members throughout the crusade city to join a two-thousand voice choir. He often used the antiphonal effect between the large choir and the great crowds which attended the meetings. His faithful trombone was always at his side and was used to accompany the congregational singing. "After thirty minutes under the sway of Rodeheaver," writes Mendell Taylor, "the atmosphere was ripe for the solo and the message."[31]

At invitation time, Rodeheaver would lead the choir in singing "Softly and Tenderly," Billy Sunday's favorite hymn. The words of the song reaffirmed the invitational appeal made by the evangelist. Nightly, hundreds would respond by "hitting the sawdust trail."

Billy Graham's song leader, Cliff Barrows (1923–   ), patterns his style after Homer Rodeheaver. (Interviewed by this writer, Mr. Barrows mentioned that he had read all of Rodeheaver's books on the practical aspects of choir directing and the leading of congregational singing.[32] He even used a trombone as accompaniment until the 1957 New York Crusade.)

The size of the Graham crusades, and the amount of preparation that must go into each, compel Barrows to select his music three weeks to a month in advance. Crusade choirs of up to five thousand or more people are formed, and practice begins several weeks prior to a crusade opening. Music has to be assembled and in the hands of choir members on the first day of practice.

Until the Billy Graham crusades became televised events, Barrows usually conducted a twenty- to thirty-minute song service of congregational singing and choir numbers. Today, each meeting includes only one or two congregational selections. The choir, likewise, has been limited to a single hymn. At least two solos are included in each meeting, one sung by Myrtle Hall and another by a guest soloist. A musical offertory is played by Tedd Smith during the collection. George Beverly Shea brings a quiet solo immediately preceding Mr. Graham's message. His solo serves as a transition from the song service into the message.

At the invitation, the choir is called upon to sing softly, "Just As I Am," accompanied by Tedd Smith at the piano and John Innes or Don Hustad at the organ. This hymn and "Almost

Persuaded" are the only two invitational hymns used. They are also the two songs that were sung at the Mordecai Ham tent meeting in 1934 when Graham made his commitment to Christ.[33]

For a number of years the entire congregation sang the invitational hymn, until Bev Shea suggested that the choir alone handle the assignment. Shea remembered how he, as an eighteen-year-old lad, was convicted by the Spirit as a choir sang "Just As I Am." He felt the effects of a soft choir number could be used by God to touch people's hearts. One day he said to Billy:

> Have you ever thought of saying, "As the choir sings, you come?" With just the choir singing there might be more contemplation upon the Holy Spirit's call. Soon after that, for the first time in his growing ministry, he began to say at the close of every service, "As the choir sings, you come!"[34]

The Functions of Music in Evangelistic Preaching

Historically, music has played an important role in drawing men to the Savior. Today's gospel music continues to be an effective tool in the ministry of evangelistic preaching, helping in a number of ways to bring people to a saving knowledge of Jesus Christ.

First, gospel music can be used to attract non-Christians to an evangelistic or worship service. Commenting on Charles Wesley's use of music, Richard Eastcott noted back in 1793, "It has been said, and I believe with great truth, that many of the converts among the Methodists have declared that the singing was their primary attraction."[35] Moody once said of his own evangelistic meetings, "The people come to hear Sankey sing and then I catch them in the gospel net."[36] Charles Alexander's song service lasted a full hour, but people would still arrive early to begin singing before the scheduled meeting time.[37]

Every evangelist in the past one hundred years has learned to depend on the drawing power of music to attract a crowd. William T. Ellis, the authorized biographer for Billy Sunday, described music's influence on Sunday's meetings:

> The tabernacle music in itself is enough to draw the great throngs which nightly crowd the building. The choir furnished not only the melodies but also a rare spectacle. . . . Without his choir Sunday could scarcely conduct his great campaigns.[38]

The same could be said about Billy Graham. How many people are attracted to Mr. Graham's crusades because of the musical program? Certainly George Beverly Shea, Myrtle Hall, Norma Zimmer, Evie Tornquist Karlsson, B. J. Thomas, Johnny Cash, and the host of other Christian musicians who have appeared on a crusade platform have influenced thousands of non-Christians to attend the evangelistic services. The crusade choir is also a stimulus which attracts many people— Christian and non-Christian alike—to the crusade. As one attendee at the 1981 Greater Baltimore Billy Graham Crusade said, "I would have attended each service just to hear that magnificent five-thousand voice choir, it was so inspiring."[39]

Music's ability to attract cannot be overstated. Once people are in a meeting, they come under another important function of music: to prepare the hearts of listeners for the entrance of the gospel. John F. Wilson asserts that music creates in the non-believer "a readiness of mind which will prepare him for a soul response to the message. . . . This is the greatest ministry music can render to one who has not yet responded to the message of salvation."[40] Dwight L. Moody understood the effective use of music in this respect. Although he could not sing a note on key, he used music in his mass campaigns because of its ability to condition a crowd.[41] Similarly, Billy Graham remarks, "We allow adequate time for the music for two reasons: (1) the people enjoy it, and expect it; (2) music, reverently rendered, creates an atmosphere for the evangelistic sermon."[42]

People's hearts must be prepared for the preaching of the Word. Men and women, their minds bombarded all day long with temporal problems, worries, frustrations, and many other things of the world, bring negative elements into an evangelistic service. Often they are physically tired and mentally worn out from an exhausting day at home, in the office, in school, or on the road. If the Word of God is successfully to penetrate their minds and hearts, the perplexities of life must temporarily be removed. An enthusiastic song service helps divert the attention of weary souls away from the problems they face to focus their thoughts on the things of God. As Cliff Barrows has written, "God has given the evangelistic song leader and the gospel singer the privilege of preparing the soil of the heart for the message of the Word of God."[43]

If the "cares of the world" are not adequately removed, Jesus said the Word of God would be choked and no fruit produced (Matthew 13:22). Barrows feels that one way to overcome the negative attitudes that people bring into the service is to stimulate the audience to participate in hearty congregational singing. He says: "When people sing together, it lifts them up. It helps them to forget their troubles as the 'things' of life fade into the background. It gives them an awareness of the presence and power of God's Spirit."[44]

How music can prepare a heart to receive God's Word is vividly illustrated in the testimony of the baseball evangelist, Billy Sunday. In the autumn of 1887, his heart was melted by the testimonies and music of some personal workers from the famed Pacific Garden Mission. He tells his own story:

> I walked down a street in Chicago in company with some ball players who were famous in the world. . . . It was Sunday afternoon and we got tanked up and then

went and sat down on a corner.... Across the street a
company of men and women were playing on instruments
... and others were singing the gospel hymns that I used
to hear my mother sing back in the log cabin in Iowa and
back in the old church where I used to go to Sunday
School.

And God painted on the canvas of my recollection and
memory a vivid picture of the scenes of other days and
other faces.

I sobbed and sobbed and a young man stepped out and
said, "We are going down to the Pacific Garden Mission.
Won't you come?"

I arose and said to the boys, "I'm through. I am going to
Jesus Christ. We've come to a parting of the ways."

I turned and left that little group on the corner ... and
walked to the little mission and fell on my knees and stag-
gered out of sin and into the arms of the Savior.[45]

Music effectively presented, be it a solo, a choir number, or
congregational singing, has the power to take one's mind off
the temporal and turn it toward God. Music is a tool to prepare
human hearts.

A third purpose of music in an evangelistic program is to
prepare the heart of the evangelist or pastor to preach the message and give the invitation. "Singing Sam" Raborn, who for a
number of years was a soloist for Dr. R. A. Torrey, had a habit
of singing only two verses of a given gospel song prior to the
message. He wanted to allow Dr. Torrey as much time as possible to preach the sermon. On one occasion, after singing only
two verses of "Somebody Cares," Torrey rose and asked him,
"Isn't there another verse to that hymn?" Sam replied, "Yes,
sir. But I did not want to take your time because I know the
people want to hear you speak." The great evangelist thirstily
said, "But my soul needs inspiring also, and that song thrills
my soul, so come back and sing the other verse."[46]

Prior to and during a worship service, the mind of the

preacher is cluttered with a thousand and one things. He, too, needs to have his heart prepared. Music is a means of ministering to the man of God. George Beverly Shea once commented about Billy Graham's need in this area: "Billy looks forward to the solo before the message as a time for people to quiet down and for him to gather strength."[47]

Fourth, music can persuasively deliver the Word of God. Songs which contain the *kērygma* can bring people to Christ as effectively as a sermon. In many ways they may do a better job, since music touches the heart and emotions. For this reason, James A. Stewart, one of Scotland's great preachers, has said: "Oftentimes . . . when a sermon fails to touch hearts, a gospel song will win them. I am a great believer in the power of song and music in the hands of holy men and women of God."[48] Ira Sankey quotes Dr. Pentecost as saying, "I have known a hymn to do God's work in a soul when every other instrumentality has failed."[49] Likewise, Donald Hustad, an accomplished musician and a professor of music, believes that throughout the ages "the Spirit of God has used the . . . 'gospel in song,' as surely as the word of preaching, to win the lost."[50] It is said that Gipsy Smith not only preached powerfully, but "sang sinners into heaven" as well. He combined a ministry of music with a ministry of evangelism. Billy Sunday once commented, "When you get to heaven you'll find that not all have been preached there. They have been sung there."[51]

If music has the power to win people to Christ, it is important that songs be selected which contain the gospel message. This is not an easy task, according to Merrill Dunlop, who served as a pianist for evangelists Jimmie Johnson and John Haggai. He says the hardest songs to find are those on the finished work of Christ.[52] It should be the prayer of Christians everywhere that God raise up song writers to compose songs whose central theme is the death, burial, and resurrection—the *kērygma*—of Jesus Christ.

Finally, music can aid non-believers at the invitation to surrender their lives to Christ. Many songs were written for the express purpose of being used as invitation hymns. Ralph Carmichael's song, "The Savior Is Waiting," is a good example. While serving as minister of music at the Temple Baptist Church in downtown Los Angeles, California, Carmichael was asked by Dr. J. Lester Harnish, the senior pastor, to write an invitational hymn. Carmichael recalls the circumstances:

> Doc called me in one day and asked for a new song which our ladies' trio would sing each night before a series of protracted meetings.... He was the speaker, and he asked for a song that could be sung after each sermon. He wanted to just back away from the pulpit and have the trio step up to the microphone and sing.[53]

As Carmichael searched his soul and God's Word for an idea, his mind was drawn back over the years to his youth. He remembers:

> Time will never fade the image I carry in my mind's eye of the picture that hung on the wall of my Sunday School room depicting the Savior standing patiently outside a closed door with His hand posed for a gentle knock. He will knock and He will wait, but He will never come in unless He's invited.

The outcome was one of this century's greatest invitational hymns:

> The Savior is waiting to enter your heart.
> Why don't you let Him come in?
> There's nothing in this world to keep you apart.
> What is your answer to Him?
>
> If you'll take one step t'ward the Savior, my friend,
> You'll find His arms open wide.
> Receive Him and all of your darkness will end.
> Within your heart He'll abide.

Chorus:
Time after time He has waited before
And now He is waiting again
To see if you're willing to open the door.
Oh, how He wants to come in!

Another hymn written specifically for the invitation is "One, Somebody, You" by Judy Moore.[54] It was composed for use by Dr. W. A. Criswell, who often issues his final appeal by saying, "While we sing this song, make your decision for Christ . . . a family—you . . . a couple—you . . . or just one, somebody—you." This invitational hymn has become a favorite among the members at First Baptist Church of Dallas, Texas.

By far the most popular and widely-used invitational hymn is Charlotte Elliott's "Just As I Am." Written in 1836, the hymn is based on Dr. Caesar Malan's exhortation to Miss Elliott twelve years earlier. The noted Swiss evangelist told the young lady, "You must come to Christ just as you are." She never forgot those words which changed her life. Kenneth W. Osbeck says of the hymn, "Without question, this hymn has touched more hearts and influenced more people for Christ than any other song ever written."[55] After her death in 1871, over a thousand letters were discovered among her papers from individuals throughout the world stating the song had profoundly affected their lives.

"Just As I Am" has become one of the trademarks of Billy Graham's ministry. When the crusade choir begins to sing the familiar lyrics, the people in the audience know it is time to make their peace with God. Cliff Barrows told this writer, "I feel that this hymn was given by God to Charlotte Elliott to touch people's lives around the world."[56]

Scores of other invitation hymns could be mentioned. (For a list of some of the most popular, see Appendix.) It is not as important which particular song is used as it is to choose a song that reinforces the appeal made by the evangelist. Every verse of a good invitation hymn will issue a call for sinners to make an immediate decision for Christ. Through the hymn the non-believer is repeatedly exhorted to come to Christ. The key ingredient the pastor or evangelist will want to look for in a hymn he is considering for the invitation is drawing power.

Music is not essential to the invitation. Thousands of gospel invitations have been given without a closing hymn. During his 1966–1967 Earl's Court Crusade in London, England, Billy Graham used no invitational hymns. Prior to the opening of the crusade, a prominent newspaper man wrote that people came forward because of the emotional appeal of "Just As I Am" instead of the message. Before long, other columnists were printing the same charges. On opening night, at the close of his message, Billy turned to Cliff Barrows and told him that no music was to be used during invitation time. For one whole month, he issued his appeal without the aid of music. As the invitation was given each night, silence filled the air as Mr. Graham stepped back and waited for the response. Sometimes for as long as thirty seconds there was not a sound. Then could be heard throughout that huge arena the squeaking of seats; only a few at first, but soon hundreds were getting up and coming forward to make their public commitment to Jesus Christ. At the close of the crusade, the reporter who originally made the accusation said, "Give us back 'Just As I Am.' The silence is too emotional!"[57]

While music is not a necessity at invitation time, it serves to enhance and adorn the commitment to Christ. It creates an atmosphere conducive to surrender. Ralph Carmichael conveyed to this author his feelings about the proper selection of invitational music:

> I have found that in those kind of quiet moments when the pastor or evangelist is offering the members of his congregation the opportunity to choose between life and death, the careful choice of a proper piece of music sung

in a reverent manner can be used most effectively by the Holy Spirit.[58]

Tom Bledsoe, song leader for the Billy Graham associate evangelists, likens invitational music to a wedding march.[59] It is not absolutely necessary, but it certainly enhances the bride coming down the aisle to meet her bridegroom. The wedding march makes the occasion more beautiful and memorable. It also serves as a signal to the bridegroom, attendants, and invited guests that the bride is coming forward to give her life to her new husband. In a similar fashion, the invitational hymn adorns this moment of surrender, and signals all concerned that the time has come for the ones whom God has called to be the Bride of Christ to give themselves to the Bridegroom.

11

Inviting Children to Christ

Children can be reached with the gospel of Jesus Christ. One children's worker calls the mass of pre-adolescent youths "the world's most fruitful mission field."[1] An evangelical researcher estimates that eighty-six percent of all converts to Christ are won before their fifteenth birthday.[2] Many para-church organizations such as Child Evangelism Fellowship, Pioneer Girls, Christian Service Brigade, Awana, and Word of Life exist for the sole purpose of winning each generation of children to the Savior. Unfortunately, a growing number of denominations have abandoned this vast mission field. The church needs to be called back to child evangelism!

The Gospel Appeal to Children

Because pre-adolescent youths are intellectually, emotionally, and socially immature, the minister of the gospel must realize that evangelism among this group is an extremely delicate process. Most children can be easily manipulated into making shallow or even pseudo-commitments to Christ. Through the use of peer pressure, the promise of rewards, or the inward desire to please the Christian worker, unwary children are often cajoled into quasi-conversion experiences. Such unscriptural methods can lead to undesirable consequences, and sometimes hinder children from making a legitimate decision for Christ in later years. Inadequately-trained youth workers, despite good intentions, often do more harm than good.

The fact that child evangelism has been the victim of abuses does not suggest that it should be abandoned. To the contrary; Jesus said, "Suffer the *little* children to come unto me, and forbid them not; for of such is the kingdom of God" (Mark 10:14). On another occasion, He admonished the disciples with these words: "Except ye be converted, and become as *little* children, ye shall not enter into the kingdom of heaven" (Matthew 18:3). Likewise, the Apostle Paul reminded Timothy "that from a child thou hast known the holy scriptures, which are able to make thee wise unto salvation . . ." (2 Timothy 3:15).

Charles Haddon Spurgeon, considered by many to be Britain's greatest expository preacher, believed a child only five years of age could receive Christ as Savior.[3]

Most developmental psychologists agree that between the ages of five and nine a child begins to develop a conscience, which enables him internally to distinguish between right and wrong. While there is no consensus among psychologists as to what *exact* age this capacity appears (for it differs with each child), it is generally agreed that the conscience is fully operational prior to the teenage years. This observation has significant theological implications. As Dr. Cos Davis concludes, "If a child has reached the stage of maturity where he is morally responsible, he is also accountable to God for his sins."[4]

History confirms that pre-adolescent children can be effectively evangelized and won to Christ. Jonathan Edwards, leader of the Great Awakening, was only seven years old when he was converted. Corrie ten Boom and Ruth Graham each came to Christ at the age of five. Evangelist Leighton Ford was also converted at five. Ford's biographer records the eventful day:

> The children . . . filed into a house at Canadian Keswick for Frances Thomas' daily "Happy Hour." Five-year-old

Leighton, a bit taller and thinner than most, took his place on the front row.

Amid her flannelgraph, chalkboard, and colorful teaching accoutrements the former missionary to China held the youngsters spellbound with the story of Nicodemus, that distinguished Jewish teacher who once asked Jesus, "How can a man be born when he is old?" And then, as she did after each meeting at Keswick, Miss Thomas asked the children to raise their hands if they wanted to respond to God's invitation for salvation. Leighton's hand shot up.

"No, Leighton," Miss Thomas whispered. "You're too young. Please be still."

Again she gave the invitation and again Leighton raised his hand. She tried once more to dissuade him.

The third time Leighton's hand was raised Miss Thomas perceived that the boy of five had understood and was prepared to make a commitment to the Savior.[5]

Leighton Ford's conversion was real. God used the faithful efforts of a former missionary to win the lad to Christ. Today Leighton Ford is an internationally-known evangelist and vice president of the Billy Graham Evangelistic Association.

Effective evangelization of children is possible. Truly the harvest is great.

How to Present the Message to Children

Children come into a saving relationship with Christ the same way that adults do. All must hear the gospel and then personally respond in repentance and faith. There are not two gospels—one for children and one for adults. The message is universal in its application. The content of the gospel is the death, burial, and resurrection of Jesus Christ. Apart from these facts, there is no gospel.

Many pastors, evangelists, and youth workers make a grave mistake in trying to lead a child to Christ without presenting the *kērygma*. They wrongly assume that the message is too difficult for a small child to comprehend. By leaving out the essentials of the substitutionary atonement and resurrection of Jesus, the Christian worker inadvertently eliminates the entire basis upon which one can be saved. No child can experience salvation without coming face to face with the Cross.

Others leave out the gospel because they refuse to believe that children are sinners, accountable before God; hence, they feel there is no need for preaching the Cross. In one major denominational study, a group of churchmen concluded that children could not be lost before sixteen years of age![6]

Regardless of man's opinion, leaving out the gospel content from the evangelistic presentation is not an option. The gospel alone is the power of God unto salvation (Romans 1:16).

The problem the Christian worker faces is not, "Should I preach the *kērygma?*", but "How can I put the gospel in terms that a child can understand?" The first obstacle, therefore, facing the preacher is a theological language barrier.

Since children think in concrete terms, it is necessary to rephrase words of an abstract nature in one's vocabulary. Such words and phrases as sin, conviction, crucifixion, resurrection, Holy Ghost, repentance, faith, blood of the lamb, give your life to Christ, admit you are lost, come to Jesus, washed in the blood, ask Christ to save you, invite Christ into your heart, make a stand for Christ and so forth, usually need re-defining for the uninitiated minds of children.

Everyone can relate to the frustration children must experience when confronted with these "unknown tongues." How common it is for one to visit a physician, medical specialist, or lawyer, and then walk out of the office not understanding what was said by the expert. Davis observes:

> This is the same type of confusion a child faces when we assume that he will understand what we intend to communicate by religious words. Just because he nods approval of what we say does not mean that he understands.[7]

As one former children's evangelist related to this writer, "If you tell them [children] that Jesus 'shed' His blood, they will think His blood is in the shed—out back of the house."[8] He further shared the following true story:

> If you tell [children] to let Jesus come into their heart, they may think that a grown man must actually fit into the heart. This happened to me when I first began teaching children. . . . A young man came up to me after [the meeting] . . . and called me a liar. He said, "What you are teaching is a bunch of lies. I just came out of science class, and there is no way a grown man can fit into my heart."[9]

To a child's literal mind, "Make a stand for Christ" might mean to build a lemonade or snowball stand for Jesus. "Washed in the blood" could bring frightening images to his naive consciousness. And what would such words as "Holy Ghost" and "lost" signify to a six-year-old?

Abstract language must be concretely defined and illustrated to the satisfaction of the child. What good does it do to use correct terminology if no one understands? Terms like sin, atonement, and resurrection must be translated into the language of children.

Every gospel message directed at children should begin with the fact of God's love. Children should be assured that God loves them, cares for them, and wants to be their friend forever. They should be taught that God is their creator. He made them. He is responsible for their existence. Most children will have no problem with these basic concepts.

Next, the issue of sin must be presented. This is a more difficult concept to explain, but it can be dealt with adequately. When speaking to a child about sin, do not use such examples as adultery, murder, and rape. Although these are real sins, they do not relate to the child's own experience. Rather speak of lying, kicking, biting, disobeying mother, grabbing toys or books out of baby brother's hands, selfishness, fighting, or throwing a temper tantrum when not getting one's own way. These are sins a child understands because they are acts of rebellion he commits daily.

The child also needs to understand that sin is an act he commits against God as well as against his parents, siblings, and friends. Sin is his choosing to do what he wants to do when God wants him to do something else.

It should then be explained that sin leads to a drastic consequence—punishment. The child must understand that his sins will not go unpunished (Romans 6:23). Just as his parents punish him for his rebellion, so must God punish him. This retribution does not negate God's love toward the child, any more than his parents' acts of discipline negate their love toward him.

The preacher can now deliver the crux of his message, the gospel of Jesus Christ. It is important to explain to children that while sin must be punished, God loves them and does not desire to see them suffer sin's consequences. Therefore, God left heaven, came to earth, took on a human body, and died in their place. God personally took their punishment.

The substitutionary atonement needs to be clearly presented to the children. If explained in concrete terms (word pictures), children can understand this great truth. Many church-affiliated publishing houses and para-church organizations have printed materials to help the youth worker effectively deliver the gospel message. Child Evangelism Fellowship produces a variety of flannelgraph lessons that clearly explain in children's language the substitutionary death of Christ on the cross. Bible Visuals, Inc. has produced a series of illustrated Bible lessons, visual aids, and object lessons like the famous Wordless Book to help the Christian worker effectively teach the gospel to children.

Sometimes a simple illustrative story can drive home to the hearts of children the biblical truths of the atonement:

"The Boy Who Lost His Boat"

Tom carried his new boat to the edge of the river. He carefully placed it in the water and slowly let out the string. How smoothly the boat sailed! Tom sat in the warm sunshine admiring the little boat that he had built.

Suddenly a strong current caught the boat. Tom tried to pull it back to shore, but the string broke. The little boat raced downstream.

Tom ran along the sandy shore as fast as he could. But his little boat soon slipped out of sight. All afternoon he searched for the boat. Finally, when it was too dark to look any longer, Tom sadly went home.

A few days later, on the way home from school, Tom spotted a boat just like his in a store window. When he got closer, he could see—sure enough—it was *his!*

Tom hurried to the store manager: "Sir, that's *my* boat in your window! I made it!"

"Sorry, son, but someone else brought it in this morning. If you want it, you'll have to buy it for one dollar."

Tom ran home and counted all his money. Exactly one dollar! When he reached the store, he rushed to the counter. "Here's the money for my boat." As he left the store, Tom hugged his boat and said, "Now you're twice mine. First, I made you and now I bought you."

Did you know that God *made* you and me and that He also *bought* us. . . .[10]

Whatever concrete method is used to communicate the gospel truth, it is imperative that children are taught an accurate concept of the Cross. As one commentator points out, the Cross is *not* God laying our sins on an innocent third party. This false interpretation caused one little girl to say, "I love Jesus, but I hate God." Children must be made to realize that it was God Himself who took their punishment.[11]

All effective gospel messages will include the truth that Jesus was raised from the dead, and as living Savior will accept us as His friend forever on the basis of His death. Children do not question the literal resurrection. They accept it as fact.

When presenting the gospel, it is wise to remember that a child's attention span is short. Do not allow the story to drag, but be enthusiastic, teach the central truth—substitutionary atonement—and repeat it often. Repetition is the key. No one is saved apart from an understanding of the Cross. Make sure you convey this truth.

The Call to Repentance and Faith

Once the gospel has been preached, the child needs to be told that God expects him to respond positively to the message. Here is where many children's workers fail. They often call upon the child to utter a prayer for salvation or to raise his hand if he wishes to receive Christ. While a child may take such actions, these movements may lull the child into a false sense of security through easy believism. The Bible is clear that before one can be converted (including a child) he must repent and believe on Christ.

Repentance. George B. Eager believes that all gospel messages to children should be followed by a call for repentance. Repentance includes an acknowledgment by the child that his sins caused God to die. He needs to realize the awesome consequences of sin; what it cost God to rescue him. A repentant heart is produced through the convicting power of the Word (Hebrews 4:12) and the Holy Spirit (John 16:8). Eager feels that repentance should be explained to children as "being sorry enough for your sins to want to stop doing them."[12]

Additionally, the child needs to understand that unless he repents, he will be held accountable for his sins. Children understand judgment more than we give them credit for.

Faith. It is easy for a child to trust Christ as his Savior. Children respond to love. Trust is ingrained in children from infancy. In fact, Dr. Erik H. Erickson, world-famous developmental psychologist, observes that the very first stage of a child's psychosocial development is that of trust.[13]

Out of necessity, a child has a built-in capacity to believe in or trust others. As Dr. Cos Davis so clearly explains:

> From the time of conception until he is grown, the child is dependent upon parents and other caregivers to do for him what he cannot do for himself. Thus, his physical, emotional, social, intellectual, and spiritual needs as a growing person dictate that he be able to trust someone else to help him in meeting these various needs. More than at any other stage or position in life, the child needs to trust others. What a tremendously important and beautiful thing to see a child's trust reinforced by those who conscientiously seek to meet his needs.
>
> As awesome as the child's need to believe is his ability to believe. He is so sure that his parents can do everything needed that it disarms and humbles us. How simple and pure is his faith! He allows adults to worry about the details of meeting his needs, and he just believes they will do it. It takes him some time to realize that the absolute faith he has in us has been somewhat misplaced. . . .
>
> One of the most sobering thoughts that could ever occupy the mind of an adult is that the child's first faith is faith in him, the parent. What an awesome responsibility to be the first object of faith for a developing life.
>
> Little children express this faith in many ways. A clap of thunder and they may rush to your arms for protection. They let you know when they are wet or soiled, with the trust you will take care of them. They simply assume that you will provide food and clothing. They also hope you will set limits to protect them from themselves and from things in the world which will harm them. All of these are expressions of the child's faith.
>
> Developmental psychologists emphasize a sense of trust as the first of the developmental tasks which the child must achieve. This trust is developed as parents meet the

basic needs of the child. For instance, feeding the child when he is hungry indicates that you care for him. He translates your response to his need into trust. At any level of development, meeting a child's needs helps him to trust you.

When one understands how the ability to trust is developed, it is not sacrilegious to say that the parent is the child's first god. Before a child ever conceives of the possibility of the idea of God, he believes only in his parents. They assume an intermediate role in his pilgrimage of faith in God.

Parents, the first object of a child's faith, influence his ability to place trust in other persons and, ultimately, in God. The healthy child is ready to form friendships and to trust significant adults, such as a teacher, pastor, or doctor. As life expands and experiences multiply, the growing child will learn to use the faith he has been taught in all types of relationships.

Hopefully, there will come a time when this faith in parents will enable the child to place his faith in Jesus as Savior. Without his real awareness, the child's faith has been in the process of transfer from parent to Jesus for some time. The simple, trusting faith in parents is expressed toward Jesus as God and as supreme. His growing awareness of parents as fallible people will no longer allow the child to completely trust them as God. But the transfer of this simple faith can be made to God, who is without fault. The best of parents have faults and are pleased to know that their children have put their trust in One who will not fail them.[14]

Because of a child's early capacity to trust, it is not difficult to lead him to Christ.

Through the use of a single verse, such as John 3:16, substituting the pronouns with the child's name to personalize it, the Christian worker can scripturally show the child what God expects of him:

"For God so loved *Billy,* that He gave His only begotten Son, that *if Billy* believeth in Him, *Billy* should not perish but have everlasting life."

Extending the Invitation

It is not enough to tell the child what to do, the worker must now give the child the opportunity to do it. An invitation should be extended to the child to immediately repent of his sins and trust Christ as Savior.

Here are some practical suggestions regarding the giving of the invitation. First, be forewarned that young children are susceptible to peer pressure. Usually the less aggressive children will follow the leader of the peer group. This could create a major problem. If the leader raises his hand or steps forward, many others may follow his example, resulting in pseudo-decisions. Should the leader not respond, others might do likewise, preventing some from coming to Christ who might have otherwise done so. Peer pressure can be a major hindrance to effectively inviting children to the Savior. Children want to feel part of the group; no one wants to be the oddball.

How does the Christian worker combat peer pressure? Simply by extending an invitation that is not "public" in nature. It is wise, when extending a gospel appeal to children, to have all present bow their heads and close their eyes. With no one looking around, the evangelist can ask those who wish to receive Christ to look up at him for a second and catch his attention or to simply lift their hands briefly in the air. Such a procedure eliminates peer pressure, since no one knows what the others are doing.

Second, the youth minister must be careful not to convey to the children that they should respond positively to the gospel just to please him. It is the very nature of small children to want to please adult authority figures. It is essential that their motive for coming to Christ be pure, not to gain the acceptance or approval of the Christian leader.

This enemy of child evangelism can be combated by the worker if he avoids saying such things as, "Nothing would please *me* more than for you to come to Christ." The child needs to know that the decision he is making for Christ is for his own good and is pleasing to God.

Third, the youth worker must never manipulate the child by offering rewards or special privileges in return for his decision. Some child evangelism programs are based on the reward system and promotions. One must seriously question the legitimacy of any decision that is made via inducement.

Fourth, never embarrass the child. Childhood is a critical period as far as the development of self-esteem is concerned. A call for public commitment is difficult for some children. The Christian worker must never violate a child's right to make a private commitment to God.

Finally, it is imperative that those children who raised their hands be followed up immediately, either privately after the meeting, or (as soon as feasible) through a visit to their homes. At this time, they need to be told of the necessity of sharing their commitment with others.

Childhood conversions are a real asset to the cause of Christ. Not only is a soul saved, but a lifetime is redeemed as well. Childhood conversions pave the way for years of Christian service. Childhood conversions produce Christian lives unmarred by years of gross sin. Childhood conversions result in lives freed from the fear of death (Hebrews 2:14). What a blessing a Christian worker receives when he is privileged to lead a little one to the Savior!

Appendix
Selected Invitational Hymns

Almost Persuaded (*Bliss*)
Come, Sinners, to the Gospel Feast (*C. Wesley*)
Come to the Savior Now (*Wigner*)
Come, Ye Sinners, Poor and Needy (*Hart*)
Free from the Law, O Happy Condition (*Bliss*)
Have You Any Room for Jesus? (Traditional)
I am Coming Home (*A. H. Ackley*)
I am Coming to the Cross (*McDonald*)
If You are Tired of the Load of Your Sin (*Morris*)
I Have Decided to Follow Jesus (Folk Hymn)
I Must Tell Jesus (*Hoffman*)
I Surrender All (*Van de Venten*)
Jesus, I Come (*Sleeper*)
Jesus is Calling (*Crosby*)
Jesus is Tenderly Calling Today (*Crosby*)
Jesus, the Sinner's Friend, to Thee (*C. Wesley*)
Jesus, I Will Trust Thee (*Walker*)
Just As I Am (*C. Elliott*)
Let Him In (*Atchinson*)
Lord, I'm Coming Home (*Kirkpatrick*)
Only a Step (*Crosby*)
Only Trust Him (*Stockton*)

Open Wide the Door (*Kitching*)
Pass Me Not (*Crosby*)
Room at the Cross for You (*Stanphill*)
The Savior is Waiting (*Carmichael*)
The Shepherd of Love (*Reitz*)
Sinners, Turn: Why Will Ye Die? (*C. Wesley*)
Softly and Tenderly (*Thompson*)
Somebody's Knocking at Your Door (Traditional)
Thou Didst Leave Thy Throne (*E. Elliott*)
While Jesus Whispers to You (*Witter*)
Whiter Than Snow (*Nicholson*)
Whosoever Will (*Bliss*)
Why Do You Wait? (*Root*)
Why Not Now? (*Nathan*)
You Must Open the Door (*Ogdon*)

Notes

Preface

1. C. E. Autrey, *Basic Evangelism* (Grand Rapids: Zondervan, 1959), p. 129.
2. Gerald S. Strober, *Graham: A Day in Billy's Life* (Old Tappan: Spire, 1976), p. 187.
3. G. Campbell Morgan, *Evangelism* (Grand Rapids: Baker Book House, 1976), p. 71.

Chapter 1

1. John R. W. Stott, *The Preacher's Portrait* (Grand Rapids: Eerdmans, 1961), p. 55.
2. Ibid., p. 55.
3. James A. Stewart, *Evangelism Without Apology* (Grand Rapids: Kregel, 1960), p. 35.
4. C. H. Dodd, *The Apostolic Preaching and Its Developments* (Grand Rapids: Baker Book House, 1980), p. 7.
5. Ibid.
6. Dodd, p. 17.
7. Ibid., p. 7.
8. Robert Mounce, *The Essential Nature of New Testament Preaching* (Grand Rapids: Eerdmans, 1960), p. 42.
9. Ibid.
10. Charles Haddon Spurgeon, *The Soul Winner* (Grand Rapids: Eerdmans, 1963), pp. 21, 22.

11. Joseph H. Thayer, *Thayer's Greek-English Lexicon of the New Testament* (Nashville: Broadman, 1977), p. 346.

12. Ibid.

13. Alan Richardson, ed., *A Theological Word Book of the Bible* (New York: Macmillan, 1950), p. 171.

14. Dodd, p. 8.

15. J. I. Packer, *Evangelism and the Sovereignty of God* (Downers Grove: InterVarsity Press, 1961), p. 43.

16. Dodd, p. 7.

17. G. Campbell Morgan, *Preaching* (Grand Rapids: Baker Book House, 1974), p. 12.

18. Packer, p. 44.

19. Stott, p. 35.

20. Roy J. Fish, *Giving a Good Invitation* (Nashville: Broadman, 1974), p. 9.

21. Thayer, p. 257.

22. Stewart, p. 24.

23. David Watson, *I Believe in Evangelism* (Grand Rapids: Eerdmans, 1976), p. 33.

24. Packer, pp. 58, 59.

25. Stewart, p. 25.

26. Packer, p. 64.

27. Stewart, p. 49.

28. Packer, p. 65.

29. Ibid., pp. 65, 66.

30. Stewart, p. 50.

31. Quoted in Packer, pp. 68, 69.

32. Stewart, p. 25.

33. Ibid., p. 26.

34. As quoted by Robert L. Sumner, *Biblical Evangelism in Action* (Murfreesboro: Sword of the Lord, 1966), p. 242.

35. Watson, p. 26.

36. G. Campbell Morgan, *Evangelism* (Grand Rapids: Eerdmans, 1976), p. 55.

37. Lewis A. Drummond, *Leading Your Church in Evangelism* (Nashville: Broadman, 1975), p. 25.

38. Kenneth S. Wuest, *Wuest's Word Studies,* Vol. III, *Untranslatable Riches* (Grand Rapids: Eerdmans, 1970), p. 31.

39. As quoted in Stephen F. Olford, *The Secret of Soul Winning* (Chicago: Moody, 1963), p. 5.

40. In Olford, p. 5.

41. Morgan, *Evangelism,* p. 41.
42. Ibid., p. 67.

Chapter 2

1. James H. Jauncey, *Psychology for Successful Evangelism* (Chicago: Moody Press, 1972), p. 17.
2. John R. W. Stott, *The Preacher's Portrait* (Grand Rapids: Eerdmans, 1961), p. 57.
3. Roy J. Fish, *Giving a Good Invitation* (Nashville: Broadman, 1974), p. 10.
4. James A. Stewart, *Evangelism Without Apology* (Grand Rapids: Kregel, 1960), p. 39.
5. Fish, p. 9.
6. John Henry Jowett, *The Preacher: His Life and Work* (Grand Rapids: Baker Book House, 1968), p. 171.
7. Joseph H. Thayer, *Thayer's Greek-English Lexicon of the New Testament* (Nashville: Broadman, 1977), p. 405.
8. Roland Q. Leavell, *Evangelism: Christ's Imperative Commission,* revised by Landrum P. Leavell II and Harold T. Bryson (Nashville: Broadman, 1979), p. 47.
9. Quoted in George Sweeting, "Why Repentance is Crucial," *Moody Monthly,* November 1977, pp. 79–85.
10. Derek Prince, *Repent and Believe* (Fort Lauderdale: Derek Prince, n.d.), p. 11.
11. J. I. Packer, *Evangelism and the Sovereignty of God* (Downers Grove: InterVarsity, 1961), p. 112.
12. Prince, p. 16.
13. Ibid., p. 13.
14. G. Campbell Morgan, *Evangelism* (Grand Rapids: Baker Book House, 1976), p. 82.
15. Kenneth S. Wuest, *Wuest's Word Studies,* Vol. III, *Studies in the Vocabulary of the Greek New Testament* (Grand Rapids: Eerdmans, 1945), p. 29.
16. Alan Richardson, ed., *A Theological Word Book of the Bible* (New York: Macmillan, 1950), p. 75.
17. Wuest, p. 29.
18. Packer, p. 71.

19. Francis A. Schaeffer, *Basic Bible Studies* (Wheaton: Tyndale House, 1972), p. 53.
20. A. T. Robertson, *Word Pictures in the New Testament,* Vol. IV (Nashville: Broadman, 1931), p. 390.
21. Robert D. Brinsmead, *The Way of Salvation* (Fallbrook: New Reformation Fellowship, 1977), p. 26.
22. Donald Grey Barnhouse, *How God Saves Men* (Philadelphia: The Bible Study Hour, 1955), p. 20.
23. Derek Prince, *Foundation for Faith* (Fort Lauderdale: Derek Prince, n.d.), p. 39.
24. Ibid., p. 29.
25. Barnhouse, p. 20.

Chapter 3

1. Joseph H. Thayer, *Thayer's Greek-English Lexicon of the New Testament* (Nashville: Broadman, 1977), p. 610.
2. Letter to author dated August 24, 1981.
3. Kenneth O. Peterman, "The Gift of Exhortation" (PhD dissertation, California Graduate School of Theology, 1980), p. 31.
4. Samuel Fisk, *The Public Invitation: Is it Scriptural? Is it Wise? Is it Necessary?* (Brownsburg: Biblical Evangelism, 1970), p. 11.
5. L. R. Scarborough, *With Christ After the Lost,* revised and expanded by E. D. Head (Nashville: Broadman, 1952), p. 145.
6. Quoted in Fisk, p. 16.
7. Letter to author dated August 1, 1981.
8. William R. Newell, *Confessing Christ* (Leesburg: The Great Commission Prayer League, 1975), p. 7.
9. John R. W. Stott, *Basic Christianity* (Grand Rapids: Eerdmans, 1971), p. 116.
10. Quoted in Bernhard Lohse, *A Short History of Christian Doctrine* (Philadelphia: Fortress Press, 1966), p. 165.
11. Newell, p. 4.
12. James H. Jauncey, *Psychology for Successful Evangelism* (Chicago: Moody Press, 1972), p. 17.
13. Stott, p. 116.
14. Faris D. Whitesell, *Sixty-five Ways to Give Evangelistic Invitations* (Grand Rapids: Zondervan, 1945), pp. 14, 15.

Chapter 4

1. T. Harwood Pattison, *The History of Christian Preaching* (Philadelphia: American Baptist Publication Society, 1903), pp. 60, 61.

2. Ibid., p. 71.

3. Robert H. Glover, *The Progress of Worldwide Missions,* revised and enlarged by J. Herbert Kane (New York: Harper and Row, 1960), p. 26.

4. Mendell Taylor, *Exploring Evangelism* (Kansas City: Beacon Hill, 1964), p. 95.

5. L. M. Perry and J. R. Strubhar, *Evangelistic Preaching* (Chicago: Moody Press, 1979), p. 44.

6. Taylor, p. 83.

7. Pattison, pp. 108, 109.

8. Perry and Strubhar, p. 45.

9. Quoted in Perry and Strubhar, p. 45.

10. Fred Barlow, *Profiles in Evangelism* (Murfreesboro: The Sword of the Lord, 1976), p. 70.

11. Jonathan Edwards, *The Works of President Edwards,* vol. 3 (New York: Leavitt, 1851), pp. 238, 239.

12. Howard G. Olive, "The Development of the Evangelistic Invitation" (ThM thesis, Southern Baptist Theological Seminary, 1958), p. 15.

13. Quoted in Taylor, p. 394.

14. Ibid., p. 397.

15. Ibid.

16. Quoted in Barlow, p. 213.

17. Ibid., p. 35.

18. Olive, pp. 16, 24.

19. Ibid., p. 25.

20. Ibid.

21. C. E. Autrey, *Basic Evangelism* (Grand Rapids: Zondervan, 1959), p. 130.

22. Henry B. McLendon, "The Mourner's Bench" (ThD dissertation, Southern Baptist Theological Seminary, 1902), p. 16.

23. Robert I. Devin, *A History of Grassy Creek Baptist Church* (Raleigh: Edward Broughton, 1880), p. 69.

24. Glover, p. 60.

25. Barlow, p. 52.

26. Quoted in Taylor, pp. 281, 282.

27. McLendon, pp. 11–15.

28. Quoted in McLendon, p. 13.

29. McLendon, pp. 7, 8.
30. Ibid., p. 10.
31. Taylor, p. 419.
32. McLendon, p. 30.
33. Olive, p. 42.
34. Bennet Tyler, *Memoirs of the Life and Character of Reverend Asahel Nettleton* (Boston: n.p., 1856), p. 100.
35. Autrey, p. 131.
36. Barlow, p. 27.
37. Gordon Lindsay, *Men Who Changed the World,* vol. 6 (Dallas: Christ for the Nations, 1979), p. 28.
38. Roland Q. Leavell, *Evangelism: Christ's Imperative Commission,* revised by Landrum P. Leavell II and Harold T. Bryson (Nashville: Broadman, 1979), p. 89.
39. Letter to author dated March 25, 1981.
40. Eric W. Hayden, *Searchlight on Spurgeon* (Pasadena: Pilgrim, 1973), pp. 7, 8.
41. Quoted in Hayden, p. 130.
42. Taylor, p. 462.
43. Roy J. Fish, *Giving A Good Invitation* (Nashville: Broadman, 1974), p. 16.
44. Taylor, p. 463.
45. A. P. Fitt, *The Life of D. L. Moody* (Chicago: Moody Press, n.d.), pp. 103, 104.
46. Ibid., p. 135.
47. John Kent, *Holding the Fort* (London: Epworth House, 1978), p. 171.
48. Fitt, pp. 146, 147.
49. Sam P. Jones, *Sermons* (New York: Wilbur B. Ketcham, 1886), pp. 242, 243.
50. Ibid., pp. 208, 209.
51. George T. B. Davis, *Torrey and Alexander* (New York: Fleming H. Revell, 1905), pp. 199–202.
52. James A. Stewart, *Evangelism Without Apology* (Grand Rapids: Kregel, 1960), p. 106.
53. Quoted in Barlow, pp. 169, 170.
54. Homer Rodeheaver, *Twenty Years With Billy Sunday* (Winona Lake: Rodeheaver-Hall-Mack, 1936), p. 127.
55. D. Bruce Lockerbie, *Billy Sunday* (Waco: Word, 1965), p. 11.
56. Elijah P. Brown, *The Real Billy Sunday* (New York: Fleming H. Revell, 1914), p. 146.
57. Lockerbie, p. 62.

58. Taylor, p. 534.
59. William T. Ellis, *Billy Sunday: The Man and His Message* (n.p.: L. T. Myers, 1914), p. 158.
60. Statement by Everett Mitchell to Robert Schuster, September 17, 1980, Tape #T1, Collection 140, Archives of the Billy Graham Center, Wheaton, Illinois.
61. Roger F. Campbell, *They Call Him The Walking Bible* (Nashville: Action Books, 1977), pp. 156, 166, 167.
62. Ibid., p. 111.
63. Luis Palau, *The Luis Palau Story,* as told to Jerry B. Jenkins (Old Tappan: Fleming H. Revell, 1980), p. 11.
64. Ibid., p. 123.
65. Information obtained from Evangelist Luis Palau, personal interview, Washington, D.C., February 5, 1981.
66. Lewis Sperry Chafer, *True Evangelism* (Grand Rapids: Zondervan, 1919), p. 20.

Chapter 5

1. Billy Graham, *Billy Graham Talks to Teen-Agers* (Wheaton: Miracle Books, 1958), p. 11.
2. John Pollock, *Crusaders: Twenty Years with Billy Graham* (Minneapolis: World Wide, 1969), pp. 8, 9.
3. Ronald C. Paul, *Billy Graham—Prophet of Hope* (New York: Ballantine, 1978), p. 37.
4. Glenn Daniels, *Billy Graham—The Man Who Walks with God* (New York: Paperback Library, 1961), p. 41.
5. Pollock, *Crusades,* p. 25.
6. Stanley High, *Billy Graham* (New York: McGraw-Hill, 1956), p. 138.
7. Paul, p. 57.
8. Howard G. Olive, "The Development of the Evangelistic Invitation" (ThM thesis, Southern Baptist Theological Seminary, 1958), p. 50.
9. *Mid-Century Crusade,* Grace Films, 1950, Film #F104, Collection 54, Archives of the Billy Graham Center, Wheaton, Illinois.
10. Pollock, *Crusades,* p. 79.
11. *The Canvas Cathedral,* Grace Films, 1949, Film #F1, Collection 74, Archives of the Billy Graham Center, Wheaton, Illinois.
12. David Poling, *Why Billy Graham?* (Grand Rapids: Zondervan, 1977), p. 18.

13. *New York Crusade,* Grace Films, 1957, Film #F40, Collection 113, Archives of the Billy Graham Center, Wheaton, Illinois.

14. *Melbourne Crusade,* Grace Films, 1959, Film #F18, Collection 113, Archives of the Billy Graham Center, Wheaton, Illinois.

15. *Greater Southern California Crusade,* World Wide Pictures, 1963, Film #F15, Collection 113, Archives of the Billy Graham Center, Wheaton, Illinois.

16. John Pollock, *Billy Graham, Evangelist to the World* (New York: Harper and Row, 1979), p. 300.

17. High, p. 90.

18. Information obtained from Dr. Graham, personal interview, Baltimore, Maryland, June 9, 1981.

19. Billy Graham, *The Challenge* (Garden City: Doubleday, 1969), pp.17; 36, 37; 69, 70; 87, 88; 119, 120; 155, 156.

20. Ibid., p. 17.

21. Billy Graham, "Insights to the Invitation," *Proclaim,* October, 1977, p. 5.

22. Gerald S. Strober, *Graham: A Day in Billy's Life* (Old Tappan: Spire Books, 1976), p. 188.

23. Billy Graham and others, *America's Hour of Decision* (Wheaton: Van Kampen Press, 1951), p. 138.

24. Donald Allen Waite, "The Evangelistic Speaking of Billy Graham" (PhD dissertation, Purdue University, 1961), p. 210.

25. Graham, *The Challenge,* p. 32.

26. Ibid., p. 68.

27. Graham and others, *America's Hour of Decision,* p. 126.

28. Nationwide telecast of the 1981 San Jose Crusade.

29. Graham, *The Challenge,* p. 33.

30. Iain Murray, *The Invitation System* (London: The Banner of Trust, 1967), pp. 3–7.

31. Quoted in Pollock, *Crusades,* p. 210.

32. Personal interview, Baltimore, Maryland, June 9, 1981.

33. High, p. 67.

34. Personal interview, Baltimore, Maryland, June 9, 1981.

35. Graham, "Insights to the Invitation," p. 5.

36. High, pp. 50, 51.

37. Quoted in Paul, p. 189.

38. Quoted in High, p. 19.

39. Quoted in Pollock, *Crusades,* pp. 22, 23.

40. Billy Graham, "Conversion—A Personal Revolution," *The Ecumenical Review,* July, 1967, p. 281.

41. Quoted in Pollock, *Crusades,* p. 275.
42. Quoted in High, p. 60.
43. Ibid., p. 57.
44. Pollock, *Crusades,* p. 54.
45. Quoted in Paul, p. 189.
46. Pollock, *Evangelist,* p. 103.
47. Waite, pp. 128, 129.
48. Quoted in Pollock, *Crusades,* p. 26.
49. Personal interview, Baltimore, Maryland, June 9, 1981.
50. G. Campbell Morgan, *Evangelism* (Grand Rapids: Baker Book House, 1976), p. 58.
51. Quoted in Strober, p. 103.
52. Quoted in Pollock, *Crusades,* p. 289.
53. Quoted in Alan Levy, *God Bless You Real Good* (New York: Essandess, 1969), p. 50.
54. Pollock, *Crusades,* p. 35.
55. Quoted in Poling, p. 154.
56. Quoted in Levy, p. 50.
57. Quoted in Pollock, *Crusades,* p. 56.
58. A. T. Robertson, *Word Pictures in the New Testament,* Vol. 4 (Nashville: Broadman, 1932), p. 168.
59. Quoted in Levy, p. 50.
60. Quoted in Pollock, *Evangelist,* p. 120.
61. Quoted in Pollock, *Crusades,* p. 31.
62. Pollock, *Evangelist,* p. 120.

Chapter 6

1. Eric Fife, "D. Martyn Lloyd-Jones: Twentieth-Century Puritan," *Eternity,* November, 1981, pp. 29, 30.
2. D. Martyn Lloyd-Jones, *Preaching and Preachers* (Grand Rapids: Zondervan, 1971), p. 271.
3. Ibid., p. 271.
4. Ibid., p. 272.
5. Ibid., p. 273.
6. Ibid., p. 274.
7. Leighton Ford, *The Christian Persuader* (New York: Harper and Row, 1966), p. 120.
8. Lloyd-Jones, pp. 274, 275.

9. Ibid., p. 275.

10. Ibid., p. 276.

11. Ibid., p. 277.

12. C. E. Autrey, *Basic Evangelism* (Grand Rapids: Zondervan, 1959), p. 128.

13. Lloyd-Jones, p. 278.

14. J. I. Packer, *Evangelism and the Sovereignty of God* (Downers Grove: InterVarsity, 1961), pp. 22, 25.

15. Stephen F. Olford, *The Christian Message for Contemporary Man* (Waco: Word, 1972), p. 54.

16. Billy Graham, *Biblical Invitations* (Minneapolis: Billy Graham Evangelistic Association, n.d.), pp. 18, 19.

Chapter 7

1. Stephen F. Olford, *The Christian Message for Contemporary Man* (Waco: Word, 1972), p. 54.

2. Letter to author from Dr. C. Sumner Wemp, Vice President of Spiritual Affairs, Liberty Baptist College, August 20, 1981.

3. Letter to author from Dr. I. D. E. Thomas, senior pastor, First Baptist Church of Maywood, California, August 1, 1981.

4. Information obtained from Dr. Charles Stanley, personal interview, Washington, D.C., January 26, 1981.

5. G. Campbell Morgan, *Evangelism* (Grand Rapids: Baker Book House, 1976), p. 65.

6. Letter to author dated August 28, 1981.

7. Quoted in William R. Moody, *The Life of Dwight L. Moody* (Murfreesboro: The Sword of the Lord, n.d.), p. 489.

8. R. G. Lee, "Why I Extend The Gospel Invitation," *The Sword of the Lord,* November 13, 1981, p. 6.

9. Letter to author from Dr. Robert L. Sumner, managing editor, *The Sword of the Lord,* July 30, 1981.

10. George E. Sweazey, *Effective Evangelism* (New York: Harper and Row, 1953), p. 44.

11. W. E. Grindstaff, *Ways to Win* (Nashville: Broadman, 1957), p. 187.

12. Billy Graham, "Conversion—A Personal Revolution," *The Ecumenical Review,* July, 1967, p. 276.

13. Ibid., p. 277.

14. John R. Rice and Robert J. Wells, eds., *How To Have A Revival* (Wheaton: The Sword of the Lord, 1946), pp. 186, 187.
15. John R. Rice, *The Evangelist* (Murfreesboro: The Sword of the Lord, 1968), p. 103.
16. Ibid.
17. Letter to author dated July 30, 1981.
18. Faris D. Whitesell, *Sixty-five Ways to Give Evangelistic Invitations* (Grand Rapids: Zondervan, 1945), p. 19.
19. Russell Blowers, senior pastor, East 91st Street Christian Church, in an address ("All Things Are Ready") at Greater Baltimore Billy Graham Crusade ministers' meeting, Baltimore, Maryland, January 8, 1981.
20. Letter to author dated August 24, 1981.
21. Letter from Dr. Helmut Thielicke to Billy Graham, trans. by Darrell Likens Guder, August 23, 1963.

Chapter 8

1. Andrew W. Blackwood, *The Fine Art of Preaching* (Grand Rapids: Baker Book House, 1976), p. 125.
2. Ozora S. Davis, *Principles of Preaching* (Chicago: University of Chicago Press, 1924), p. 217.
3. L. R. Scarborough, *With Christ After the Lost,* revised and expanded by E. D. Head (Nashville: Broadman, 1952), p. 146.
4. Charles W. Koller, *Expository Preaching Without Notes* (Grand Rapids: Baker Book House, 1962), p. 19.
5. Personal interview, Baltimore, Maryland, June 10, 1981.
6. Ken Anderson, *Hallelujah Harry* (Chicago: Pacific Garden Mission, 1977), p. 22.
7. Charles H. Spurgeon, *Lectures to My Students* (Grand Rapids: Baker Book House, 1977), p. 148.
8. Scarborough, p. 116.
9. Charles H. Spurgeon, *The Soul Winner* (Grand Rapids: Eerdmans, 1963), p. 94.
10. Quoted in Curtis Hutson, "Evangelistic Preaching" (Decatur: Forest Hills Baptist Church, n.d.), p. 15.
11. Personal interview, Baltimore, Maryland, June 9, 1981.
12. C. E. Autrey, *Basic Evangelism* (Grand Rapids: Zondervan, 1959), p. 127.
13. Blackwood, p. 10.

14. Quoted in Thomas Cook, *Soul Saving Preaching* (London: Charles H. Kelly, n.d.), p. 65.
15. J. I. Packer, *Evangelism and the Sovereignty of God* (Downers Grove: InterVarsity, 1961), p. 50.
16. James H. Jauncey, *Psychology for Successful Evangelism* (Chicago: Moody Press, 1972), p. 102.
17. Quoted in Lloyd M. Perry and John Strubhar, *Evangelistic Preaching* (Chicago: Moody Press, 1979), p. 130.
18. Quoted in Robert L. Sumner, *Evangelism: The Church on Fire* (Murfreesboro: The Sword of the Lord, 1960), p. 166.
19. Lewis A. Drummond, *Leading Your Church in Evangelism* (Nashville: Broadman, 1975), p. 51.
20. Spurgeon, *The Soul Winner,* p. 26.
21. Ibid., p. 84.
22. Quoted in Andrew W. Blackwood, *The Preparation of Sermons* (New York: Abingdon-Cokesbury, 1948), p. 170.
23. Blackwood, *The Preparation,* p. 170.
24. Spurgeon, *The Soul Winner,* p. 75.
25. Quoted in Bailey E. Smith, *Real Evangelism* (Nashville: Broadman, 1978), p. 36.
26. Ibid.
27. Quoted in John Pollock, *Crusades: Twenty Years with Billy Graham* (Minneapolis: World Wide, 1969), p. 150.
28. Autrey, p. 133.

Chapter 9

1. David Poling, *Why Billy Graham?* (Grand Rapids: Zondervan, 1977), p. 34.
2. Leroy Patterson, "Is the Altar Call a Sacred Cow?", *Eternity,* n.d., p. 3. (Reprint.)
3. Ibid., pp. 3, 4.
4. William R. Moody, *The Life of Dwight L. Moody* (Murfreesboro: The Sword of the Lord, n.d.), p. 145.
5. Ibid.
6. A. P. Fitt, *The Life of D. L. Moody* (Chicago: Moody Press, n.d.), p. 78.
7. D. Martyn Lloyd-Jones, *Preaching and Preachers* (Grand Rapids: Zondervan, 1971), p. 276.

8. Information obtained from taped "Invitation Service" conducted by W. A. Criswell, pastor of First Baptist Church of Dallas, Texas, November 25, 1979.

9. Charles W. Koller, *Expository Preaching Without Notes* (Grand Rapids: Baker Book House, 1962), p. 106.

10. Letter to author dated August 20, 1981.

11. Andrew W. Blackwood, *Evangelism in the Home Church* (New York: Abingdon-Cokesbury, 1942), p. 135.

12. Charles H. Spurgeon, *The Soul Winner* (Grand Rapids: Eerdmans, 1963), pp. 42, 43.

13. James A. Stewart, *Evangelism Without Apology* (Grand Rapids: Kregel, 1960), p. 109.

14. "No Regrets," *Daily Blessing,* vol. 15, no. 2, June 24, 1973.

15. Rex Humbard, "The Night John Dillinger Came Forward," *Answer,* n.d., p. 32.

16. Testimony by Jerry Falwell, pastor, in an address ("We're Going to Look Like Jesus") at the National Religious Broadcasters' Convention, Washington, D.C., January 27, 1981.

17. Moody, p. 163.

Chapter 10

1. Donald P. Ellsworth, *Christian Music in Contemporary Witness* (Grand Rapids: Baker Book House, 1979), p. 27.

2. James Sallee, *A History of Evangelistic Hymnody* (Grand Rapids: Baker Book House, 1978), p. 9.

3. Ellsworth, p. 31.

4. Ibid., pp. 29, 30.

5. Roland Q. Leavell, *Evangelism: Christ's Imperative Commission,* revised by Landrum P. Leavell II and Harold T. Bryson (Nashville: Broadman, 1979), p. 68.

6. George W. Stansbury, "The Music of the Billy Graham Crusades, 1947–1970: An Analysis" (DMA dissertation, Southern Baptist Theological Seminary, 1971), p. 10.

7. Quoted in Ellsworth, pp. 49, 50.

8. Sallee, pp. 22, 23.

9. Ibid., pp. 12, 15.

10. Both hymns quoted in Ellsworth, p. 67.

11. Sallee, p. 14.

12. Ellsworth, p. 69.
13. Mendell Taylor, *Exploring Evangelism* (Kansas City: Beacon Hill, 1964), p. 266.
14. Ellsworth, pp. 69, 73.
15. Emory Stevens Bucke, ed., *The Methodist Hymnal* (Nashville: The Methodist Church, 1966), pp. 111, 118.
16. Ellsworth, p. 71.
17. Sallee, p. 44.
18. Quoted in Sallee, p. 44.
19. John F. Wilson, *An Introduction to Church Music* (Chicago: Moody Press, 1965), p. 57.
20. Quoted in Donald P. Hustad, ed., *Hymns for the Living Church* (Carol Stream: Hope, 1974), pp. 231, 254.
21. Quoted in Sallee, p. 63.
22. Quoted in Kenneth W. Osbeck, *Singing with Understanding* (Grand Rapids: Kregel, 1979), p. 22.
23. Sallee, p. 38.
24. A. P. Fitt, *The Life of D. L. Moody* (Chicago: Moody Press, n.d.), p. 88.
25. Ibid., p. 109.
26. Ira D. Sankey, *My Life and Story of the Gospel Hymns* (New York: Harper and Brothers, 1906), pp. 268–277.
27. Phil Kerr, *Music in Evangelism* (Glendale: Gospel Music, 1939), p. 94.
28. Osbeck, p. 22.
29. Sallee, p. 65.
30. George T. B. Davis, *Torrey and Alexander* (New York: Fleming H. Revell, 1905), p. 145.
31. Taylor, p. 532.
32. Taped interview, Greenville, South Carolina, September 20, 1981.
33. Ibid.
34. "George Beverly Shea: Just As He Is," *In Tune,* Summer, 1981, p. 15.
35. Quoted in Ellsworth, p. 72.
36. Quoted in Taylor, p. 514.
37. Stansbury, p. 95.
38. William T. Ellis, *Billy Sunday: The Man and His Message* (n.p.: L. T. Myers, 1914), p. 263.
39. Statement by Thomas Wilkerson, businessman, personal interview, Baltimore, Maryland, June 14, 1981.
40. Wilson, p. 19.
41. Ellsworth, p. 93.
42. Quoted in Loren R. Williams, "The Evangelist and Revival Music," *The Church Musician,* March, 1959, p. 7.

43. Cliff Barrows, "Music in Evangelism," *Decision,* December, 1962, p. 12.

44. Quoted in Stansbury, p. 86.

45. Quoted in Ellis, pp. 40, 41.

46. Barlow, p. 140.

47. Quoted in Alan Levy, *God Bless You Real Good* (New York: Essandess, 1969), p. 33.

48. James A. Stewart, *Evangelism Without Apology* (Grand Rapids: Kregel, 1960), p. 95.

49. Quoted in Sankey, p. vi.

50. Quoted in Stansbury, p. 196.

51. Quoted in Ellis, p. 262.

52. Interview with Merrill Dunlop by Robert Schuster, June 1, 1979, Tape #2B, Collection 50, Archives of the Billy Graham Center, Wheaton, Illinois.

53. Quoted in David Swaney, ed., *Ralph Carmichael: A Portrait* (Newbury Park: Lexicon Music, 1977), pp. 8–11.

54. Judy Moore, "One, Somebody, You?" (Grand Rapids: Singspiration, 1978), pp. 2–4.

55. Osbeck, p. 181.

56. Barrows, taped interview.

57. Ibid.

58. Letter to author dated December 3, 1981.

59. Personal interview, Baltimore, Maryland, June 10, 1981.

Chapter 11

1. George B. Eager, *How To Succeed in Winning Children to Christ* (Valdosta, Georgia: The Mailbox Club, 1979), p. 3.

2. Ibid., p. 3.

3. Ibid., p. 4.

4. Cos H. Davis, Jr., *Children and the Christian Faith* (Nashville: Broadman Press, 1979), p. 13.

5. Norman B. Rohrer, *Leighton Ford: A Life Surprised* (Wheaton: Tyndale House, 1981), p. 26.

6. Eugene Chamberlain, *When Can a Child Believe?* (Nashville: Broadman Press, 1973), p. 34.

7. Davis, p. 61.

8. Richard Haynes, "Winning Children to Christ," Unpublished manuscript, November 1983, p. 1.
9. Ibid., p. 1.
10. "The Boy Who Lost His Boat," Good News Publishers, Westchester, Illinois, n.d.
11. Ibid., p. 18.
12. Ibid., p. 24.
13. Evelyn M. Duvall, *Family Development* (Philadelphia: J. B. Lippincott, 1971), p. 134.
14. Davis, pp. 32–34.

Bibliography

BOOKS

History of Evangelism

Cole, Edward B. *The Baptist Heritage.* Elgin: David C. Cook, 1976.
Dodd, C. H. *The Apostolic Preaching and its Developments.* Grand Rapids: Baker Book House, 1980.
Glover, Robert H. *The Progress of Worldwide Missions,* revised by J. Herbert Kane. New York: Harper and Row, 1960.
Hefley, James C. *God Goes to High School.* Waco: Word, 1970.
Pattison, T. Harwood. *The History of Christian Preaching.* Philadelphia: American Baptist Society, 1903.

Evangelism: Theory and Practice

Autrey, C. E. *Basic Evangelism.* Grand Rapids: Zondervan, 1959.
Barnhouse, Donald Grey. *How God Saves Men.* Philadelphia: The Bible Study Hour, 1955.
Bavinck, J. H. *An Introduction to the Science of Missions,* translated by David H. Freeman. Philadelphia: Presbyterian and Reformed, 1960.
Biederwolf, William E. *Evangelism: Its Justification, Its Operation and Its Value.* New York: Fleming H. Revell, 1921.
Bisagno, John R. *The Power of Positive Evangelism.* Nashville: Broadman, 1968.
Borchert, Gerald L. *Dynamics of Evangelism.* Waco: Word, 1976.
Chafer, Lewis Sperry. *True Evangelism.* Grand Rapids: Zondervan, 1919.

BIBLIOGRAPHY

Dobbins, Gaines S. *Good News to Change Lives.* Nashville: Broadman, 1976.

Ferm, Robert O. *The Psychology of Christian Conversion.* Westwood: Fleming H. Revell, 1959.

Finney, Charles G. *Revivals of Religion.* Virginia Beach: CBN University Press, 1978.

———. *Revival Fire.* Minneapolis: Bethany Fellowship, n.d.

Fisk, Samuel. *Divine Sovereignty and Human Freedom.* Neptune: Loizeaux, 1973.

Fletcher, Lionel B. *Effective Evangelism.* London: The Religious Tract Society, n.d.

Ford, Leighton. *The Christian Persuader.* New York: Harper and Row, 1966.

Goodell, Charles L. *Pastoral and Personal Evangelism.* New York: Fleming H. Revell, 1907.

Griffin, Emory A. *The Mind Changers.* Wheaton: Tyndale House, 1976.

Grindstaff, W. E. *Ways to Win.* Nashville: Broadman, 1957.

Hutson, Curtis. *Winning Souls and Getting Them Down the Aisle.* Murfreesboro: The Sword of the Lord, 1978.

Jauncey, James H. *Psychology for Successful Evangelism.* Chicago: Moody Press, 1972.

Krupp, Nate. *A World to Win.* Minneapolis: Bethany Fellowship, 1966.

Leavell, Roland Q. *Evangelism: Christ's Imperative Commission,* revised by Landrum P. Leavell II and Harold T. Bryson. Nashville: Broadman, 1979.

Martin, Robert J. *All About Witnessing.* Grand Rapids: Baker Book House, 1975.

Morgan, G. Campbell. *Evangelism.* Grand Rapids: Baker Book House, 1976.

Olford, Stephen F. *The Christian Message for Contemporary Man.* Waco: Word, 1972.

———. *The Secret of Soul Winning.* Chicago: Moody Press, 1963.

Outler, Albert. *Evangelism in the Wesleyan Spirit.* Nashville: Tidings, 1971.

Packer, J. I. *Evangelism and the Sovereignty of God.* Downers Grove: Inter Varsity, 1961.

Pink, Arthur W. *The Sovereignty of God.* Grand Rapids: Baker Book House, 1976.

Prince, Derek. *Repent and Believe.* Fort Lauderdale: Derek Prince, n.d.

Rice, John R. *Bible Baptism.* Murfreesboro: The Sword of the Lord, 1943.

———. *The Evangelist.* Murfreesboro: The Sword of the Lord, 1968.

Scarborough, L. R. *With Christ After the Lost,* revised and expanded by E. D. Head. Nashville: Broadman, 1952.

Smith, Bailey E. *Real Evangelism.* Nashville: Broadman, 1978.

Spurgeon, Charles H. *The Soul Winner.* Grand Rapids: Eerdmans, 1963.

Stewart, James A. *Evangelism Without Apology.* Grand Rapids: Kregel, 1960.

Stott, John R. W. *Basic Christianity.* Grand Rapids: Eerdmans, 1971.

Stott, John R. W., and others. "The Nature of Evangelism." *The Lausanne Covenant.* Minneapolis: World Wide, 1974.

Sumner, Robert L. *Biblical Evangelism in Action.* Murfreesboro: The Sword of the Lord, 1966.

Sweazey, George E. *Effective Evangelism.* New York: Harper and Brothers, 1953.

Taylor, Mendell. *Exploring Evangelism.* Kansas City: Beacon Hill, 1964.

Torrey, Reuben A. *How to Bring Men to Christ.* Minneapolis: Dimension, 1977.

————. *How to Work for Christ.* New York: Fleming H. Revell, 1901.

Watson, David. *I Believe in Evangelism.* Grand Rapids: Eerdmans, 1976.

Evangelistic Preaching

Blackwood, Andrew W. *The Fine Art of Preaching.* Grand Rapids: Baker Book House, 1976.

————. *The Preparation of Sermons.* New York: Abingdon-Cokesbury, 1948.

Broadus, John A. *A Treatise on the Preparation and Delivery of Sermons,* ed. Edwin C. Dargan. 27th ed. New York: Hodder and Stoughton, 1898.

Brooks, Phillips. *Lectures on Preaching.* Grand Rapids: Baker Book House, 1969.

Cook, Thomas. *Soul Saving Preaching.* London: Charles H. Kelly, n.d.

Davis, Ozora S. *Principles of Preaching.* Chicago: University of Chicago Press, 1924.

Fish, Roy J. *Giving A Good Invitation.* Nashville: Broadman, 1974.

Fisk, Samuel. *The Public Invitation: Is it Scriptural? Is it Wise? Is it Necessary?* Brownsburg: Biblical Evangelism, 1970.

Hutson, Curtis. "Evangelistic Preaching." Decatur: Forrest Hills Baptist Church, n.d. (Mimeographed.)

Jones, Ilion T. *Principles and Practice of Preaching.* Nashville: Abingdon, 1956.

Jowett, J. H. *The Preacher: His Life and Work.* Grand Rapids: Baker Book House, 1968.

Koller, Charles W. *Expository Preaching Without Notes.* Grand Rapids: Baker Book House, 1962.

Lloyd-Jones, D. Martyn. *Preaching and Preachers*. Grand Rapids: Zondervan, 1971.

Martin, O. Dean. *Invite*. Nashville: Tidings, 1973.

Morgan, G. Campbell. *Preaching*. Grand Rapids: Baker Book House, 1974.

Mounce, Robert. *The Essential Nature of New Testament Preaching*. Grand Rapids: Eerdmans, 1960.

Murray, Iain. *The Invitation System*. London: The Banner of Truth, 1967.

Nevin, John W. *The Anxious Bench*. 3rd ed. Reading: Daniel Miller, 1892.

Perry, Lloyd M. *Biblical Preaching for Today's World*. Chicago: Moody Press, 1973.

Perry, Lloyd M., and John R. Strubhar. *Evangelistic Preaching*. Chicago: Moody Press, 1979.

Phelps, Austin. *The Theory of Preaching*, revised and abridged by Faris Whitesell. Grand Rapids: Eerdmans, 1947.

Sargant, William. *Battle for the Mind*. New York: Doubleday, 1957.

Short, Robert. *Evangelistic Preaching*. Nashville: Tidings, 1946.

Southard, Samuel. *Pastoral Evangelism*. Nashville: Broadman, 1962.

Spurgeon, Charles H. *Lectures to My Students*. Grand Rapids: Baker Book House, 1977.

Stanfield, V. L. *Effective Evangelistic Preaching*. Grand Rapids: Baker Book House, 1965.

Stott, John R. W. *The Preacher's Portrait*. Grand Rapids: Eerdmans, 1961.

Whitesell, Faris D. *Sixty-five Ways to Give Evangelistic Invitations*. Grand Rapids: Zondervan, 1945.

Church Evangelism

Bisagno, John R. *How to Build an Evangelistic Church*. Nashville: Broadman, 1971.

Blackwood, Andrew W. *Evangelism in the Home Church*. New York: Abingdon-Cokesbury, 1942.

Bryan, Dawson C. *Building Church Membership Through Evangelism*. Nashville: Abingdon, 1952.

Criswell, W. A. *Criswell's Guidebook for Pastors*. Nashville: Broadman, 1980.

Drummond, Lewis A. *Leading Your Church in Evangelism*. Nashville: Broadman, 1975.

Eerdman, Charles R. *The Work of the Pastor*. Philadelphia: Westminster, 1924.

Goodell, Charles L., and others. *The Pastor, His Own Evangelist*. Cleveland: F. M. Barton, 1911.

Graf, Arthur E. *The Church in the Community.* Grand Rapids: Eerdmans, 1965.

Rice, John R. and Robert J. Wells, eds. *How to Have a Revival.* Wheaton: The Sword of the Lord, 1946.

Sumner, Robert L. *Evangelism: The Church on Fire.* Murfreesboro: The Sword of the Lord, 1960.

Sweeting, George. *The Evangelistic Campaign.* Chicago: Moody Press, 1955.

Noted Evangelists, Past and Present

Anderson, Ken. *Hallelujah Harry.* Chicago: Pacific Garden Mission, 1977.

Barlow, Fred. *Profiles in Evangelism.* Murfreesboro: The Sword of the Lord, 1976.

Brown, Elijah P. *The Real Billy Sunday.* New York: Fleming H. Revell, 1914.

Bunyan, John. *Grace Abounding to the Chief of Sinners.* Chicago: Moody Press, 1959.

Campbell, Roger F. *They Call Him The Walking Bible.* Nashville: Action, 1977.

Davis, George T. B. *Torrey and Alexander.* New York: Fleming H. Revell, 1905.

Edwards, Jonathan. *The Works of President Edwards.* 3 vols. New York: Leavitt, 1851.

Ellis, William T. *Billy Sunday: The Man and His Message.* n.p.: L. T. Myers, 1914.

Finney, Charles G. *Memoirs of Reverend Charles G. Finney.* New York: Fleming H. Revell, 1876.

Fitt, A. P. *The Life of D. L. Moody.* Chicago: Moody Press, n.d.

Gunther, Peter F., comp. *Great Sermons by Great Preachers.* Chicago: Moody Press, 1960.

Ham, Edward E. *A Biography of Mordecai F. Ham.* Louisville: The Old Kentucky Home Revivalist, 1950.

Hayden, Eric W. *Searchlight on Spurgeon.* Pasadena: Pilgrim, 1973.

Headley, P. C. *Evangelists in the Church from Philip to Moody and Sankey.* Boston: Henry Hoyt, 1875.

Jones, Sam P. *Sam Jones' Sermons.* Chicago: Rhodes and McClure, 1886.
————. *Sermons.* New York: Wilbur B. Ketcham, 1886.

Lindsay, Gordon. *Men Who Changed the World.* 7 vols. Dallas: Christ for the Nations, 1979.

Lockerbie, D. Bruce. *Billy Sunday.* Waco: Word, 1965.

Moody, Dwight L. *Moody's Gospel Sermons,* ed. Richard S. Rhodes. Chicago: Rhodes and McClure, 1898.

Moody, William R. *The Life of Dwight L. Moody.* Murfreesboro: The Sword of the Lord, n.d.

Palau, Luis. *The Luis Palau Story,* as told to Jerry B. Jenkins. Old Tappan: Fleming H. Revell, 1980.

Rodeheaver, Homer. *Twenty Years with Billy Sunday.* Winona Lake: Rodeheaver-Hall-Mack, 1936.

Rohrer, Norman B. *Leighton Ford: A Life Surprised.* Wheaton: Tyndale House, 1981.

Talmage, T. DeWitt. *500 Selected Sermons.* 20 vols. Grand Rapids: Baker Book House, 1978.

Thornbury, John F. *God Sent Revival.* Grand Rapids: Evangelical Press, 1977.

Tyler, Bennet. *Memoirs of the Life and Character of Reverend Asahel Nettleton.* Boston: n.p., 1856.

Wiersbe, Warren W. *Listening to the Giants.* Grand Rapids: Baker Book House, 1980.

————. *Walking with the Giants.* Grand Rapids: Baker Book House, 1976.

Works by and about Billy Graham

Blewett, Bob, and Lois Blewett. *Twenty Years Under God,* ed. George M. Wilson. Minneapolis: World Wide, 1970.

Burnham, George. *Billy Graham: A Mission Accomplished.* Old Tappan: Fleming H. Revell, 1955.

Daniels, Glenn. *Billy Graham: The Man Who Walks with God.* New York: Paperback Library, 1961.

Gillenson, Lewis W. *Billy Graham and Seven Who Were Saved.* New York: Pocket Books, 1968.

Graham, William Franklin. *Biblical Invitations.* Minneapolis: Billy Graham Evangelistic Association, n.d.

————. *Billy Graham Talks to Teen-agers.* Wheaton: Miracle, 1958.

————. *The Challenge.* Garden City: Doubleday, 1969.

————. *How to be Born Again.* Waco: Word, 1977.

————. *You Have to Choose.* Minneapolis: Billy Graham Evangelistic Association, 1980.

Graham, William Franklin, and others. *America's Hour of Decision.* Wheaton: Van Kampen, 1951.

High, Stanley. *Billy Graham.* New York: McGraw-Hill, 1956.

Levy, Alan. *God Bless You Real Good.* New York: Essandess, 1969.

Mitchell, Curtis. *Those Who Came Forward.* Philadelphia: Chilton, 1966.

Paul, Ronald C. *Billy Graham—Prophet of Hope.* New York: Ballantine, 1978.

Poling, David. *Why Billy Graham?* Grand Rapids: Zondervan, 1977.

Pollock, John. *Billy Graham, Evangelist to the World.* New York: Harper and Row, 1979.

————. *Crusades: Twenty Years with Billy Graham.* Minneapolis: World Wide, 1969.

Strober, Gerald S. *Graham: A Day in Billy's Life.* Old Tappan: Spire, 1976.

White, John Wesley. *Everywhere Preaching the Gospel.* Minneapolis: Billy Graham Evangelistic Association, 1969.

Evangelism and Music

Blackwell, Lois S. *The Wings of the Dove.* Norfolk: Donning, 1978.

Bucke, Emory Stevens, ed. *The Methodist Hymnal.* Nashville: The Methodist Church, 1966.

Ellsworth, Donald P. *Christian Music in Contemporary Witness.* Grand Rapids: Baker Book House, 1979.

Eskew, Harry, and Hugh McElrath. *Sing with Understanding.* Nashville: Broadman, 1980.

Hustad, Donald P., ed. *Hymns for the Living Church.* Carol Stream: Hope, 1974.

Kent, John. *Holding the Fort.* London: Epworth, 1978.

Kerr, Phil. *Music in Evangelism.* 3rd ed. Glendale: Gospel Music, 1950.

Lorenz, Ellen Jane. *Glory, Hallelujah.* Nashville: Abingdon, 1980.

Osbeck, Kenneth W. *Singing with Understanding.* Grand Rapids: Kregel, 1979.

Sallee, James. *A History of Evangelical Hymnody.* Grand Rapids: Baker Book House, 1978.

Sankey, Ira D. *My Life and Story of the Gospel Hymns.* New York: Harper and Brothers, 1906.

Swaney, David, ed. *Ralph Carmichael: A Portrait.* Newbury Park: Lexicon Music, 1977.

Terry, Lindsay. *How to Build an Evangelistic Church Music Program.* Nashville: Thomas Nelson, 1974.

Wilson, John F. *An Introduction to Church Music.* Chicago: Moody Press, 1965.

Wohlgemuth, Paul W. *Rethinking Church Music.* Chicago: Moody Press, 1973.

Children's Evangelism

Chamberlain, Eugene. *When Can a Child Believe?* Nashville: Broadman, 1973.
Davis, Cos H., Jr. *Children and the Christian Faith.* Nashville: Broadman, 1979.
Eager, George B. *How to Succeed in Winning Children to Christ.* Valdosta: The Mailbox Club, 1979.

DISSERTATIONS AND THESES

Baird, John E. "The Preaching of William Franklin Graham." PhD dissertation, Columbia University, 1959.
Girtman, Harry Spruiell. "The Preaching of William Frank 'Billy' Graham." ThM thesis, Southern Baptist Theological Seminary, 1955.
McLendon, Henry B. "The Mourner's Bench." ThD dissertation, Southern Baptist Theological Seminary, 1902.
Olive, Howard G. "The Development of the Evangelistic Invitation." ThM thesis, Southern Baptist Theological Seminary, 1958.
Peterman, Kenneth O. "The Use of the Gift of Exhortation." PhD dissertation, California Graduate School of Theology, 1981.
Stansbury, George W. "The Music of the Billy Graham Crusades, 1947–1970: An Analysis and Evaluation." DMA dissertation, Southern Baptist Theological Seminary, 1971.
Tilden, Philip Nelson. "Classical Elements of Persuasion Used by Billy Graham during the San Francisco Bay Area Crusade." ThM thesis, Golden Gate Baptist Theological Seminary, 1961.
Waite, David Allen. "The Evangelistic Speaking of Billy Graham, 1949–1959." PhD dissertation, Purdue University, 1961.

PERIODICALS

Barrows, Cliff. "Musical Evangelism." *The Church Musician,* October, 1963, pp. 6–9.

————. "Music in Evangelism." *Decision,* December, 1962, pp. 11–13.

Fife, Eric. "D. Martyn Lloyd-Jones: Twentieth-Century Puritan." *Eternity,* November, 1981, pp. 29–31.

Firebaugh, Glenn. "How Effective Are Citywide Crusades?" *Christianity Today,* March 27, 1981, pp. 24–29.

"George Beverly Shea: Just As He Is." *In Tune,* Summer, 1981, pp. 15–18.

Graham, William Franklin. "Conversion—A Personal Revolution." *The Ecumenical Review,* July, 1967, pp. 271–284.

————. "Insights into the Invitation." *Proclaim,* October, 1977, pp. 4, 5.

Houston, Tom. "Preaching to the People of Luke's Time Today." *Christianity Today,* May 29, 1981, pp. 22–25.

Humbard, Rex. "The Night John Dillinger Came Forward." *Answer,* n.d., p. 32.

Jones, Bruce W. "Evangelism Is. . . ." *The Standard,* December, 1979, pp. 16, 17.

Maxwell, L. E. "A Good Confession." *Biblical Research Monthly,* June, 1981, p. 25.

"No Regrets." *Daily Bread,* June 24, 1973, p. 102.

Olford, Stephen F. "No Invitation Without Proclamation." *Moody Monthly,* September, 1979, pp. 81–83.

Patterson, Leroy. "Is the Altar Call a Sacred Cow?" *Eternity* (reprint), pp. 1–4.

Patterson, Vernon W. "The Prayer Heard Around the World." *Decision,* October, 1975, pp. 3, 12.

Shea, George Beverly. "How God Uses A Song." *Decision,* February, 1961, p. 16.

Sweeting, George. "Why Repentance IS Crucial." *Moody Monthly,* November, 1977, pp. 79–85.

Williams, Loren R. "The Evangelist and Revival Music." *The Church Musician,* March, 1959, p. 7.

Wirt, Sherwood E. "High Trails." *Decision,* September, 1974, pp. 4–7.

Newspapers

Appelman, Hyman. "God's Last Call." *The Sword of the Lord,* December 26, 1980.

Lee, R. G. "Why I Extend The Gospel Invitation." *The Sword of the Lord,* November 13, 1981.

Shuler, Phil. "The Delight of the Invitation." *The Biblical Evangelist,* June, 1975.

Smith, Gipsy. "Don't Be Afraid of the Cross." *Vision,* August–September, 1979.
Smith, Oswald J. "When the Harvest is Past." *The Sword of the Lord,* June 5, 1981.

Index

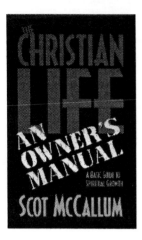

The Christian Life: An Owner's Manual

Scot McCallum

This college and adult-level resource provides both the open-minded unbeliever and the believer new in the Christian life with a reader-friendly guide to the basics of Christian belief.

3194-8 • 144 pp.

Free and Clear: Understanding and Communicating God's Offer of Eternal Life

R. Larry Moyer

"This book is for any pastor or layperson who takes the Great Commission seriously. . . . I think you'll come away with a fresh appreciation for the salvation we have in Christ, and a renewed desire to present the gospel to others." —Luis Palau

3177-8 • 304 pp.

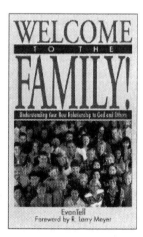